BEST
FURNITURE
BUYING TIPS
EVER!

BEST
FURNITURE
BUYING TIPS
EVER!

JENNIFER LITWIN

HOUSE OF COLLECTIBLES

NEW YORK TORONTO LONDON SYDNEY AUCKLAND

House of Collectibles and colophon are registered trademarks of Random House, Inc.

RANDOM HOUSE is a registered trademark of Random House, Inc.

This book is available for special discounts for bulk purchases for sales promotions or premiums. Special editions, including personalized covers, excerpts of existing books, and corporate imprints, can be created in large quantities for special needs. For more information, write to Special Markets/Premium Sales, 1745 Broadway, MD 6-2, New York, NY, 10019 or E-mail *specialmarkets@randomhouse.com*.

Please address inquiries about electronic licensing of any products for use on a network, in software, or on CD-ROM to the Subsidiary Rights Department, Random House Information Group, fax 212-572-6003.

Visit the House of Collectibles Web site:
www.houseofcollectibles.com.

Library of Congress Cataloging-in-Publication data is available.

ISBN: 0-375-72111-8

Acknowledgments

Best Furniture Buying Tips Ever! is the culmination of many people's efforts. I want especially to thank my agent, Linda Loewenthal of the David Black Literary Agency, for her undying support and creativity where this book was concerned. Linda, you have been a most loyal advocate and friend.

Next, I would like to thank the team at Random House for believing in and working so hard to create this book. Sheryl Stebbins, Dorothy Harris, and the rest of the team working with me at Random House have been a joy to collaborate with, and are truly the most creative group I could imagine in the publishing world.

There are so many other people who have been inspirational to me as I generated ideas for this book. Ellen Blackman, you are not only my publicist—and the very best publicist I have ever met at that—but also a creative thinker who always thinks outside the box and comes up with truly original ideas.

I also owe a huge thanks to Bob Lang, who took my passion for wanting to help consumers buy furniture and channeled that passion into a book proposal that made sense.

Cheri Gogo has been enormously helpful to me in researching furniture topics. Cheri, I owe a big thanks to you for always searching out new information.

I also want to thank the American Furniture Manufacturer's Alliance and the American Home Furnishings Association for providing me with industry surveys. And I want to thank Patti Freeman, a retail analyst at Jupiter Research Company, for providing me with results for some of the surveys conducted by Jupiter.

A special thanks to the interior designers and furniture designers interviewed throughout this book, who have shared with me their wisdom and ideas about styles, trends, and saving money. Thank you to the furniture designers for providing their own personally designed furniture for the cover of the book; I am so proud to show off your innovative designs.

And finally, thank you to my extremely supportive family—Stuart, Edward, and Bailey—for showing their interest and sharing my excitement every step along the way. You have encouraged me throughout this entire project!

Table of Contents

Introduction

1 **Jennifer's Prescription:** Insider Tips, Pitfall Alerts, and Solutions for Smart Furniture Shopping *001*

2 **Selecting Furniture:** Critical Pointers to Make You Savvy, Not Sorry *031*

3 **Raising Your Antiques IQ:** Clues that Spell "F-A-K-E" *054*

4 **Mission Impossible:** Decoding Furniture Prices *060*

5 **The Styles and the Stylish:** A History of Furniture Trends *071*

6 **From the Mouths of Experts:** Top Designers Share Their Insights and Secrets *098*

7 **Up-and-Comers:** North America's Ten Best Newly-Discovered Furniture Designers *117*

8 **Name That Furniture:** The Details Behind History's Most Famous Pieces *144*

9 **Not a Conclusion, But a Beginning . . .** *151*

Glossary *155*

Bibliography *165*

Index *167*

Photo Credits *168*

About the Author *172*

Introduction

For the majority of us, buying furniture—whether it's one particular dream piece or an entire house-ful—is not only one of the most important purchases we will ever make aside from buying our homes, but is also one of the most overwhelming and compli-cated processes we will ever experience. Prior to reading *Best Furniture Buying Tips Ever!*, you proba-bly thought that the furniture-shopping process meant having to endure countless frustrating and fruitless hours of wandering aimlessly from store to store, only to discover that you are not only unable to find the fabulous furniture you desire at the budget you can afford, but also too ill-informed and insecure even to ask the right questions about the inventory.

Who in the world are all those designers, you've won-dered, and how can I ever understand the myriad of styles and trends that are available? There is Art Deco, contemporary, antique, reproduction, mid-21st-century, and on and on. What source can I turn to that will help me figure out what to pay and where to shop for the special pieces I want, and will also give me information about all the options available so I can make informed furniture selections that are right for me? *Best Furniture Buying Tips Ever!* will provide you with everything you need to know in order to successfully master all of your furniture-shopping goals!

In this book, I simplify the entire furniture-shopping experience for you by sharing the wealth of experi-ence I have acquired over many years working in the furniture industry. I have spent more than a decade traveling around the country as a serious furniture buyer, shopping on behalf of well-known decorators and nonprofessional clients. So let's roll up our sleeves, and I'll start at the beginning by telling you my story.

Years ago when my husband, Stuart, and I bought our first home, we were in the same boat as most new shoppers furnishing their homes. Confused and in the dark, we had no idea where to buy furniture, much less what questions we should ask the dealers and salespeople or what prices we should pay. We wanted to seem like savvy shoppers, but the truth was that we knew very little about furniture and it showed. Like so many couples just starting out, we toured retail outlets and showrooms like the walking wounded on the front lines, occasionally falling back exhausted into display chairs to rest our tired feet. The dealers in the stores we visited knew that we were amateurs, and the majority of them used this to their advantage by trying to overcharge us. Perhaps even worse than the price gouging, though, were the sometimes-snobby salespeople who seemed to take great pleasure in making us feel like we were wasting their time.

My love of furniture dates all the way back to when I was a youngster exploring the great furniture pieces in my grandmother's home, dreaming about the day when I would finally grow up and select all kinds of treasures to fill my own home. When it was finally my chance to pursue this dream, however, I quickly became discouraged.

I will never forget one particularly embarrassing moment which occurred at a high-end antiques showroom in Chicago that made me feel rather like Eliza Doolittle, the ignorant flower girl from *My Fair Lady* who must acclimate herself to London's high society. When I asked the salesperson if her showroom carried anything other than English antiques, she condescendingly quipped, "We don't have any English antiques, dear. We only have French." After what seemed like the longest silence I have ever known, I realized that it was time for me to become knowledgeable about the industry if I was going to be at all successful buying furniture for my home. I also vowed that I would never again be vulnerable to dealers trying to overcharge me or falsely represent their inventories. I became committed to becoming an expert on bargaining and negotiating prices so that I could get the best deal on the furniture I wanted to buy!

At the time of this moment of truth, I was working on the trading floor of a large bank, having earned my MBA from the University of Chicago Graduate School of Business. The bank, however, was a far cry from the world of furniture. Long hours spent on the trading floor prevented me from devoting any extra time during the week to picking furniture for my home or learning anything firsthand about furnishings. So how in the world, I wondered, would I be able to transform myself from the Eliza Doolittle of furniture shopping into a savvy fine-furnishings expert? I decided to put my banking career on hold while I learned about furniture and the furniture business.

I joined the famed auction house Sotheby's as an intern to learn all I could about furniture, and working there proved an amazing experience for me in many ways. For one thing, Sotheby's served as an excellent Professor Henry Higgins to my Eliza Doolittle—a marvelous training ground that enabled my transformation by providing me with a well-rounded education about furniture and its history.

I came away from my Sotheby's experience with a passion for furniture and a hunger for a permanent career in the furniture industry. I opened my own furniture store, selling everything from antiques to contemporary furniture. Not content to sit complacently in my store all day, I found myself traveling around the country to buy inventory, and I cultivated a long list of interesting clients who hired me to help them find furniture in the course of my travels. I was extremely lucky during this period in my career, because I not only discovered that I had a wonderful eye for picking out furniture for my customers, but also quickly tapped into many terrific and unusual resources for buying furniture. To this day, many people—including interior designers—call me to help them find pieces they can't find on their own, and I love helping them.

In recent years, in addition to working with clients, I have been lecturing and teaching furniture classes in Chicago. Perhaps my most rewarding job, however, has been as a contributing writer for *Consumers Digest* magazine. Spending long hours carefully researching and reviewing furniture products for the magazine's regular *Consumers Digest* "Best Buy" feature is especially gratifying, because it goes to the core of the consumer's need to understand the complete picture before choosing to buy a particular piece of furniture. Testing countless couches, sleeper sofas, and futons is a challenging job that has given me a keen understanding of the consumer's point of view when buying furniture—and this understanding, in turn, has helped make *Best Furniture Buying Tips Ever!* the book of choice for consumers who want to master the furniture-shopping process.

My recently released book, *Furniture Hot Spots: The Best Furniture Stores and Web Sites Coast to Coast*, is the first-ever national furniture sourcebook, and is a natural complement to this book. In *Furniture Hot*

Spots, I take readers on a virtual-reality tour of hundreds of furniture stores—from antiques to contemporary, from expensive to inexpensive—and I also review Web sites and chain stores selling furniture. Through colorful and detailed store reviews, I create the feeling of actually shopping in all of the stores in the twelve U.S. cities I visited. And while *Furniture Hot Spots* gives readers a heads-up on where and how to buy really great pieces, *Best Furniture Buying Tips Ever!* completes the total picture by giving you the vital inside shopping tips that will help you make the right furniture purchases.

The furniture industry has grown exponentially over the last decade. Today the industry, with $71 billion in annual sales, presents many more shopping choices than in the past. Companies like Target and Costco have created home furnishings divisions to fill a niche in the market. Other companies, like Williams-Sonoma Home, are focusing primarily on catalog sales, and still others, like 1stdibs.com, are specializing in furniture auction Web sales. (By the way, furniture Web sales amounted to approximately $640 million in 2004, and that number is expected to double by 2008, according to a recent study conducted by *InFurniture* magazine.)

Thus, today's furniture sources have expanded to include large corporate retail stores, small independent shops, catalogs, interior decorators and designers, and the Internet. These additional shopping sources can easily overwhelm and confuse even the most determined shopper. Until recently, furniture selection on Web sites selling furniture was rather limited—in fact, 95 percent of all Web sales were comprised of purchases from Crate & Barrel, Pottery Barn, or Williams-Sonoma. Today, however, these percentages are shifting as a result of everyday newcomers entering the market and joining the Internet craze. I am pleased to see so many small businesses and manufacturers gaining a fair share of the Web sales once monopolized by retail giants.

In recent years, low interest rates have enabled consumers to purchase new homes and renovate existing properties; all of this activity in the home sector has increased the public's demand for furniture. *Best Furniture Buying Tips Ever!* arms consumers with the necessary knowledge to find and acquire the right furnishings for their homes. A recent study conducted by Jupiter Research among more than 5,000 people of all ages and socioeconomic groups demonstrated that you, the furniture buyer, want collections you can add to rather than having to buy everything at once. You desperately want to find salespeople who know about the decorating process and the products they are selling. You want retailers to provide space between furniture displays so you can inspect the individual pieces from various angles, and you prefer to see the pieces in simulated room settings. Additionally, you would like a twenty-four-hour trial period within which you can return a piece if you change your mind. You want to know what constitutes quality: Is a $5,000 sofa better than a $1,000 one? If so, why? What is an antique? Is an antique better than a reproduction? Should you view antiques as an investment? Should you hire a decorator or interior designer? How do these professionals charge for their services? *Best Furniture Buying Tips Ever!* will answer all of these questions.

Today, buying something as simple as a couch, upholstered chair, or dining table has become a complicated process because there is such a huge range of styles, quality, and pricing in the marketplace. To assist you, I review these three types of furniture pieces and discuss the primary features to which you should pay careful attention when buying such pieces in the expensive, middle-priced, and inexpensive price ranges.

Additionally, I am intrigued by the vast number of gifted furniture designers working today, especially the ones we rarely hear about. In fact, the reason so few consumers know their names is that these designers either work for high-powered designers who don't wish to share the credit or work in smaller, lesser known one-man shops. In this book, I'll provide my picks for the best up-and-coming furniture designers in America; I want you to know who these people are so you can have access to them and their work. I believe these designers are the innovators who will shape the trends and future of the furniture industry.

Elsewhere in this book, I have interviewed some of the country's best-known interior designers, many of whom have decorated the homes of the most well-known people in America, to get their views on trends and the furniture industry. I have included their tips and ideas in this book so that you may benefit from their wisdom.

Finally, I have created my Web site, www.jenniferlitwin.com, to answer E-mail questions from consumers, and I respond quickly to questions or comments. My Web site features links to over 500 furniture Web sites, ranging from antiques to contemporary, and from expensive to value-conscious, consumer polls, buyers' discounts from stores across the country that I have lobbied to get from stores, a list of hundreds of furniture stores and their descriptions, links to their Web sites and directions, a weekly cartoon that tells furniture-shopping stories—and the latest trends and interviews with furniture designers, interior designers, and retailers from across the country.

So sit down, kick back, and enjoy reading about the, until now, mysterious furniture industry. At the end of this book, you are going to be a knowledgeable consumer, and you'll never again feel inadequate when confronting snooty salespeople. Good-bye, Eliza Doolittle; hello, savvy furniture shopper!

1

Jennifer's Prescription

Insider Tips,
Pitfall Alerts,
and Solutions for
Smart Furniture
Shopping

n theory, the concept of furnishing a home is an exciting rite of passage. The notion of filling your own place with furnishings that not only make a personal statement about who you are but also about how you live is an inspiring prospect. Unfortunately for the majority of us, however, any romantic illusions we hold about furniture shopping are shattered once we visit that first showroom, and we quickly learn that the actual process of furniture shopping can be extremely stressful and mind-boggling.

Having spent years as a professional buyer, I know exactly how confusing the whole furniture-shopping process can be. The novice shopper has countless questions: How will I ever learn enough about the various kinds of furniture even to ask the right questions? Who are all these furniture designers? Should I shop with a decorator? Should I buy antiques or reproductions? What about buying at auction or online? How much is all of this going to cost me? In the end, you may feel too overwhelmed by the seemingly endless array of all of the choices and ways to buy furniture. You may even be too embarrassed to ask the salespeople the simplest questions, or you may feel bullied by dealers who either have little time to spend with you or who brush you off entirely.

For many people, the mere thought of furnishing their homes makes them feel panicky. But before you have an anxiety attack over the furniture-shopping task that lies ahead, let me assure you that this doesn't have to be the case. Why? Because I know the process, and I don't want you to have to go through all of these confusing and unsettling shopping experiences. To guarantee your success I am going to walk you through the entire process step by step. I will fully explain the many aspects of buying furniture, from selecting what kind of furniture you wish to buy (antiques, transitional, or contemporary) to understanding the construction of a piece, working with an interior designer, and understanding the frequent additional charges associated with the process—charges such as shipping and assembly, which often are not expressly discussed at the time of purchase. Best of all, I'll tell you about the many perks to which you may be entitled when buying furniture, such as free local delivery, lenient return policies, and written warranties.

Hindsight is foresight, and hearing countless horror stories from my clients over the years has taught me many essential things about the furniture-buying process. Above all, for example, I've learned the importance of acting like a strong-willed, knowledgeable consumer from the moment I open the door to any furniture store, gallery, or showroom, and from the moment I first meet with a prospective decorator. In the chapter that follows, I'll introduce you to more key pieces of furniture-shopping advice based on my own personal experiences and those shared with me by friends, clients, and consumers through the years. Many of the scenarios profiled here are common situations you may encounter on your own furniture-shopping excursions; my hope is that reading about them will prevent you from falling prey to the same types of problems on your next shopping venture. Armed with these words of caution, you'll make wiser furniture-buying decisions, save money, and in the end achieve your goal of becoming a smart and self-sufficient shopper. Let's begin!

Dealing with Furniture Dealers

In an ideal furniture world, all furniture dealers would be charming and forthright—informative people who would gladly take you around their showrooms, welcoming your questions and proudly pointing out everything there is to know about their inventories. Their information would be accurate and truthful. But although I have actually met a few memorable dealers like this over the thousands of miles I have traveled in my cross-country furniture adventures, in the real world such dealers are few and far between. While I don't want to portray all dealers as big bad wolves, I will caution you that dealers can present imposing challenges even for the most sophisticated furniture shoppers. Your attitude, knowledge, and level of confidence will play an integral role in determining how successful you will be in your interacting with them. To ensure that you have the best experience possible, keep the following tips in mind:

Negotiate with the dealer. A woman recently told me that every time she goes to a furniture store and

is about to purchase a piece of furniture, she freezes when discussing price. She is always afraid to ask for a discount, and she hopes that the dealer will simply offer her a discount without having to be asked. Needless to say, this is the wrong approach.

Most dealers will give you a discount if you just ask for one. While researching my previous book, *Furniture Hot Spots*, I attempted to negotiate furniture prices with dealers in many of the stores I reviewed. I found that in 85 percent of cases where a dealer claimed to give discounts only to the trade, that dealer would also give discounts to members of the public, if asked. Keep in mind that, if dealers are to survive our cyclical economy and the stiff competition in today's furniture industry, it is especially important for them to keep their inventories moving and to bring in fresh stock. Moreover, because dealers know that today's buyer has more options and is better-educated than ever before (thanks in part to my books!), they will often use discounts to lure customers and win future business.

When dealing with independent retailers (as opposed to chain stores, with whom negotiating generally will not work), a good rule of thumb is to ask for a 20 percent discount and see how the dealer reacts. While you can't do this with chain stores you can try this with independent retailers. Don't be shy when it comes to striking a bargain; you have nothing to lose, and lots of potential dollars to gain in savings!

Do your homework and ask the right questions. One day, while shopping at what I believed to be an upscale 20th-century furniture store in New York City, I saw some very ordinary-looking metal-and-wood chairs. On the price tag, I saw that the dealer was describing the chairs as those of George Nelson, a famous furniture designer of the 1950s and 1960s, and was charging $5,500 for the pair. Posing as a regular shopper, I asked the dealer why the price was so high. He replied that these chairs, like the rest of his inventory, were "designer" pieces, and thus warranted this price. When I then innocently asked him how he knew the chairs were George Nelson, he casually replied, "I read a lot of magazines." Not satisfied with this flippant answer, I took it a step further and asked whether he would be willing to provide me with a certificate of authenticity if I bought the chairs. When he replied with a curt "no," I immediately began to walk out of the store. The dealer quickly ran after me, yelling that he knew the chairs to be George Nelson pieces because they were signed and dated on the bottom. I knew, however, that most furniture made in the mid-20th century was neither signed nor dated—by this time in the history of furniture design, labels or metal plaques were most commonly used to identify pieces. The previous sentence suggests that the furniture dealer was lying when he said that the pieces were signed and dated on the bottom, so the pieces were fake. Now fully aware of the dealer's dishonesty, I kept on walking, having saved myself $5,500 that might otherwise have been spent on two perfectly ordinary, not-so-designer chairs.

The moral of the story? If you're unsure about the validity of a signature or the identity of a piece, don't be afraid to question a dealer or even call in an expert for a second opinion before making the final purchase. Research the type of furniture you plan to buy so you will know the right questions to ask of a dealer, and so you'll know when a dealer is trying to pull the proverbial wool over your eyes. Know the facts before you invest.

Don't get ripped off by design centers! Visiting the country's largest design centers has taught me that design centers usually have one thing in common: they cater to the designer, or trade-only, business and not the end-user. Design centers are usually large buildings or complexes made up of hundreds of showrooms. These showrooms are sometimes open for the public to view, but the public is almost never allowed to buy from them directly; generally, designers must purchase the furniture on behalf of their clients.

Recently, though, while visiting one particular city, I decided to drop in on its design center because I had been hearing so much about the improvements it had made in customer service. I was curious to see for myself how consumer-friendly it had actually become. When I met the guard at the information desk and told him I was writing this book and wanted permission to browse around the building, he immediately asked me whether I was in the design center's "club." Upon telling him that I had no idea what he meant by the "club," he informed me that the design center now had a club, and that for a flat fee of *only* $275, members of the public would be allowed to browse the building. Payment of this $275 fee, the guard also informed me, would also allow me the privilege of paying an additional fee of $90 per hour for one of the design centers on-site interior designers to escort me around its hallways, only to be able to then mark up their cost of anything I buy!

Never pay fees to a design center simply for the "privilege" of browsing. Most design centers will only allow the public to make purchases through professional interior decorators anyway. So why would you agree to pay some exorbitant amount of money just to look around, when you're not even allowed to buy anything on your own? They might as well be selling you some pricey beachfront property in Point Barrow, Alaska. More importantly, you don't need these pricey "clubs." Nowadays you can shop many of these sources online, since many manufacturers also have lines that they sell directly to the public. In fact, most design centers today allow the

public to roam their buildings for free. Never pay just to wander around! Though it's true that design centers can be a wonderful place to get decorating ideas, there are plenty of other ways for you to find decorating inspiration—without paying exorbitant fees!

Dress the part. All customers are not created equal in the eyes of a dealer. Recently, dressed in jeans and an old T-shirt, I visited a store that everybody had been raving about. I noticed that the first floor had very little furniture on display, so I asked the salesperson if there was any other furniture downstairs. "No," he replied indifferently, "this is all there is." As I turned to leave the store, I gave the man my business card and told him I was writing this book. Suddenly his entire demeanor changed: he turned red in the face and became very flustered. "Yes, we have another floor of furniture on the lower level that I would love to show you," he nervously explained. When I asked him why he hadn't told me this in the first place, he said, "I'm sorry . . . I didn't know who you were."

Wow! A Four carat diamond ring...I can charge her full retail.

The lesson here is that a dealer is likely to judge a book by its cover! Unfortunately, we live in a world where furniture dealers and sales clerks often judge shoppers based on appearance. In my case, a salesperson made a judgment based on my rugged clothing that I would be unable to afford quality furniture. As a result, that dealer lost my respect and future business.

While all customers deserve to be treated equally by a store, you may very well find yourself to be subjected to a similar experience if you're the type who loves to go shopping in your favorite old jeans and T-shirt. But keep in mind that there are dealers out there who will base price on nothing other than how much you look like you can afford to pay. Ultimately, the goal is to strike a balance between a polished appearance that commands the respect of salespeople, and a casual appearance that discourages dealers from superficially inflating their prices. When I shop, I prefer to look dressed-down but presentable, so that no one will assume I can pay higher prices based simply on what I wear.

Dealing with Interior Designers

Reality TV shows often depict interior designers as creative geniuses who, when given carte blanche, can magically transform barren houses into incredible havens in a matter of minutes. Because designers don't play that kind of role in real life, you need to be aware of some critical pointers when working with them. When working with a house's total layout and look, though, a designer will help you think of ideas that you might never have considered. It's also true that most of us are not color or fabric experts, and designers can really help to put a house together and make it look well-coordinated by selecting the right mix of patterns, colors, and textures. Designers can also help save you time simply by knowing the right places to shop. But working with designers is not always as seamless a process as television would have us believe. For this reason, you need to be aware of some critical pointers when working with them.

Choose your designer carefully. Recently I visited a newly opened shop owned by an interior designer. As I looked around the showroom, I noticed that everything was extremely overpriced and that the furniture was poorly finished, with obvious touch-ups and repairs. It appeared as though the designer was simply passing off pieces he had picked up at a resale shop.

It goes without saying that this is not the sort of designer with whom I wanted to do business, and neither should you. In fact, you should never work with any designer who can't accurately represent his or her own inventory. This includes inflated pricing or misrepresenting the goods. The best way to learn about a designer is through a word-of-mouth referral

from someone you know and whose opinion you trust. In addition, make sure the designer you choose is knowledgeable about the type of furniture you want for your home—if you want to furnish your house with antiques, for example, try to get a feel for the designer with an extensive knowledge of antique furniture. And don't be bashful about asking potential designers for references from past clients; a credible designer won't be offended or put off by such a request. You should also ask potential dealers or designers where they get their inventory; knowing where they get their goods will tell you a lot about where they will spend your money.

Use caution with custom pieces. A woman once told me that she was working with an interior designer scouting out couches. The designer suggested that, instead of shopping for a couch, they should go to the designer's upholsterer and let him design and custom-build the couch. When the couch was built, it ended up costing the woman more than $10,000. She couldn't believe how expensive it was since she knew she could have bought a comparable couch for about $3,000. Upon delivery of the couch she expressed her outrage to the upholsterer and told him that she was shocked at the high price. He asked her how much she had paid for the couch, and when she told him $10,000 he looked like he was going to faint! He told her that he had charged the designer only a fraction of that price, and couldn't believe how much the designer had marked up the couch.

Hiding behind layers of markups is one way that designers can conceal their profits, and using upholsterers and cabinetmakers is a common example of this ploy. Don't be afraid to tell a designer you want to look in stores to see if you can find something more reasonably priced before hiring an upholsterer or cabinetmaker to custom-design a piece. If you do decide to go the custom route, find out exactly what the piece will cost *before* you give the OK for the contractor to go ahead.

Set clear billing limits with your designer. My neighbor hired a decorator to help her furnish her apartment. She agreed to pay the decorator a design fee, an hourly rate, plus a percentage of the purchase price of all furniture and materials she purchased through him. When the final bill came, she almost passed out when she saw how much she had spent. The problem was this: she was unable to get the decorator to provide a detailed summary of his $15,000 bill for hours he claimed to have spent on the job. She felt that she had overspent, seen no real results, and ultimately been ripped off.

When it comes to paying a designer, stay away from non-agreed-upon expenses or open-ended hourly billing arrangements. Instead, you need to have a concrete billing arrangement that makes you both feel comfortable and leaves little room for interpretation. Designers can offer a great deal of value

when decorating, but it's important to set definite billing limits—for example, a cap on the number of hours spent on individual projects or on the entire project as a whole. Otherwise, as is the case with lawyers and other service providers who charge hourly fees, the bill can add up quickly!

A successful relationship with your designer will require trust, and a closed-end contract specifying a finite amount to be paid for his or her services will help to facilitate this. In some cases, a designer's work may be difficult to quantify, but knowing that your billing arrangement prevents your designer from taking advantage of you will help you to feel secure in your working relationship. You will want to "try each other out" for a period of time before deciding if this is the right marriage. The contract can always be modified after a period of time.

Remove incentives for your designer to overcharge. A woman once told me that her contract with her designer was structured so that the designer would get a 30 percent commission on every single furniture

purchase she made. The designer promised the woman that she would shop for furniture in all kinds of places across the country, from expensive to inexpensive venues. Most importantly, she promised not to spend a lot of time in design centers, where the furniture tends to be pricier, with custom options and hefty shipping expenses. Once the project began, however, the designer ended up spending most of her time in the most expensive showrooms at the local design center, which resulted in exorbitant commissions.

Don't allow your designer to be rewarded monetarily for him or her to choose the most expensive furniture. Make sure you arrange to pay the designer a flat fee for all furniture that will be purchased, or a percentage of the furniture's cost that is not to exceed a specified maximum amount. After all, what incentive does a designer have to seek out quality furniture at the best prices if you pay him or her a 30 percent commission on everything he or she buys, no matter what its cost? In reality, paying your designer an unlimited commission is a bit like the case of asking the fox to guard the henhouse: your designer will be faced with a conflict of interest that could easily tempt him or her to overspend.

Choose an imaginative designer whose taste reflects your own. Years ago, well before I got into the business, I worked on a project in which I needed help with fabrics and color. I decided to hire a graduate of one of the most prestigious interior design schools in the country to help me put it all together. At the conclusion of the project, however, I was disappointed. Though highly qualified on paper, the designer I had selected showed me fabrics and colors that were merely "safe"—they lacked originality and any real excitement. Although she had gone to school for many years to become a designer, she was afraid to come up with any unusual or creative ideas. It was clear that this designer was limited in her abilities as a professional because she was lacking in spirit and imagination—two intangible qualities that cannot be learned or measured, but rather must come from within the individual.

From this experience, I learned an important lesson: Select the designer whose taste most reflects your own and who you feel will be easy to work with, regardless of whether he or she went to design school.

Many designers, including one of the top designers in the country who has helped me with some of my own decorating projects, have an artistic or creative background that is much better suited to putting a beautiful room together than someone who has graduated from a fancy design school. Style and flair are something innate to a person and cannot always be taught in a school. Moreover, keep in mind that just as important as a designer's creative gifts is his or her intuitive ability to make your home reflect your true personality and lifestyle. If the end result is to be a good one, there should always be a compatibility or meeting of the minds somewhere in the creative process between decorator and client.

Caveats for Furniture Buyers

Get it in writing. A few months ago, I shopped for a piece of furniture at a reputable, well-known chain with a reputation for providing excellent service. When purchasing some chairs, I asked my salesclerk if the store offered a written warranty in case anything went wrong with my purchases. To my surprise, neither the clerk nor anyone else working in the store seemed to know whether the store offered a warranty. Only after making a harried phone call in the back room did the clerk inform me that the store did not offer such warranties, but that it did "have an excellent reputation for making it good if something breaks."

While not every reputable furniture store provides buyers with warranties, stores that offer such warranties—especially in writing—are much more likely to offer full replacement if a piece becomes damaged or broken. Some companies, like Ethan Allen, even offer full replacement for damaged or broken goods several years after your purchase. A warranty is especially important in the case of big chain stores, because it is unlikely that your salesperson will still be working at such a store if you need to return the furniture in several months or a few years. To me, providing a warranty is a sign of that a store has honorable intentions. You should always proceed with caution in the absence of a warranty—even if a salesperson professes his or her store's good intentions, as in the above example—because stores that don't provide warranties have the right to not "make good" on any future problems you may encounter with your furniture purchases.

Watch out for hidden expenses. A friend of mine recently bought a piece of furniture from a design center. At the time she purchased the furniture, she thought she was paying in full because she paid for both the piece and shipping expenses. A few weeks later, however, she got a phone call from a local shipping company, which had received the piece from another shipping company and was arranging for a time to deliver the furniture. My friend was surprised to learn that she would have to pay two shipping bills for one piece of furniture. Even worse, when the furniture arrived and she asked the delivery workers

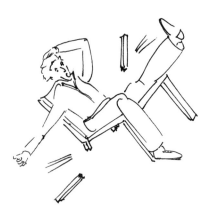

to set up the piece, they said they would only do so for yet an additional fee.

To avoid paying more than you've bargained for, know exactly what expenses are included in a piece's final price; don't allow the dealer to conceal expenses from you, only to be surprised when you get the furniture delivered or receive the final bill. When buying furniture from most showrooms in a design center, you should expect to pay two shipping bills: one for the goods to ship across the country, and the other for the goods to transport from a local warehouse in your city to your home. If you don't purchase furniture in a design center, you should only have to pay one shipping fee.

Furnish your home gradually. Before my girlfriend moved into the new house she had built, she felt the need to order enough furniture for the entire house—so that everything would look perfect, she thought, like something out of a magazine. When furniture began arriving at her new home, however, she called me in a state of panic. Some pieces were

the wrong color, others were the wrong size, and in some cases the fabrics were all wrong.

When furnishing your home, you will generally be happier with the final result if you don't rush to furnish your entire house at once. The mistakes my friend made are common, and are usually the result of trying to predict how you will use your house before you have actually lived in it. Even though we want everything to look perfect, the reality is that trends involving colors or styles will affect us. Colors, fabric, and furniture will go in and out of style, and buying everything all at once leaves no room to grow with the times. I think the result of trying to do everything all at once is that your home may look like something out of a magazine instead of like a well-functioning, livable home. Ultimately my friend had to replace most of what she had bought, because she felt that her furnishings did not fit with her family's personality and lifestyle. In the end, she paid a high price for her premature choices.

Buy antiques for love, not money. Several years ago I bought an exquisite piano bench that was over 100 years old. I spent a lot of money on this piece—a gorgeous, professional-looking Austrian bench—because I dreamt that it would inspire my children to someday become master pianists. When I realized that no one in my family wanted to play piano, I decided to sell it—but no one seemed the least bit interested in buying it. When I asked a dealer friend of mine why this was so, he told me that the bench's style was no longer desirable—that people were looking for benches that were sturdier than mine, without a swivel. So much for antiques holding their value! Luckily, I had bought the bench strictly to satisfy my vision of mothering two budding Beethovens, and not because of its resale value.

My experience with the bench taught me a valuable lesson: Buy what you like, and not what you think will bring you a return on your investment. As a friend of mine once said so accurately, "There was just as much ugly furniture as beautiful furniture designed in the 17th century"—in other words, the mere fact that a piece is old does not mean that its value or desirability will necessarily increase over time. It can be easy to forget that many variables affect the sale price of antique and contemporary furniture—such prices will always depend both on

current styles and on supply and demand, and will not necessarily increase with a piece's age.

Negotiate, negotiate, negotiate. While most chain furniture or department stores offer sales from time to time, it is often difficult to negotiate with these outlets unless there are extenuating circumstances, such as a store closing or a line of furniture being discontinued. Unfortunately, price, shipping, and other additional expenses are usually fixed and non-negotiable. On the other hand, smaller, non-corporate entities are often much more receptive to negotiating. I recently visited a great furniture store in Atlanta, and when I said that I couldn't buy the piece because I would have to take it all the way back to Chicago, the owner offered to ship the piece to me for $100. This was a terrific bargain, because other stores would have charged between $300 and 400 to ship the exact same piece!

The lesson? When visiting smaller stores, always try to negotiate price, as well as such extras as local delivery and shipping costs. These wonderful mom-and-pop-type enterprises are generally willing to go out of their way to make sure that you walk away

with a good deal. In many cases, you cannot imagine what smaller stores will do to make a sale—from offering a more flexible return policy or a certificate of authenticity to free or reduced shipping, free assembly, or flexible payment plans. Just know exactly what you are going to ask for ahead of time, and be gracious when striking a deal.

Understand how design centers work. While researching my previous book, *Furniture Hot Spots*, I traveled around the country visiting design centers. In one such design center—I don't dare mention which—I was asked to show identification before entering the premises. When I told the woman at the information desk that I was writing this book, she haughtily replied that only qualified professionals were allowed in the building. Undaunted, I marched right past her and continued on with my undercover research mission! But although I am unfazed by the often poor treatment, which will likely send chills up your spine, and confusing pricing systems at design centers—remember, I've been doing this for a long time!—you, as a nonprofessional buyer, may easily become overwhelmed, assuming that you make it inside at all.

To make your experience less intimidating, understand the pricing in design center showrooms *before* you arrive. Typically, a piece will have two separate prices: list price and net price. Net price—also known as the wholesale price—is the price a designer pays the showroom when he or she buys a piece. List price—the price that you, the end user, will ultimately pay for the piece—is the price charged to you by that same designer when he or she passes the piece along to you. The problem with list and net pricing is that each showroom offers a different discount to the trade, and the price tags are often purposely misleading or difficult to understand. If you ask a salesperson in a showroom to help you understand a piece's pricing, you will often be told that you are not entitled to know the pricing because you are only the end user. Having this experience in a showroom might seem truly humbling to you, as it once did to me. But the system is unlikely to change, as showroom employees and owners are generally so afraid of losing designer business that they go along with this system of goofy pricing and haughty service. Your best defense is to understand the system before you arrive, and don't allow yourself to be intimidated by it.

Know when your furniture will be delivered. Years ago I bought the most beautiful couches. I had waited to afford them for what seemed like forever, and then I had to wait patiently for another *six whole months* until they arrived! The showroom from which I bought them had told me to expect delivery in three to four months, but I ended up having to wait six months. I still remember all of the occasions during that waiting period when visitors to my

home had no place to sit. By the time the couches finally did arrive, I had practically forgotten what they looked like! I was furious.

When buying furniture, you should always know when you will be able to take delivery of your purchases. Delivery times can vary, and are important to ascertain up front at the time of your purchase. If taking delivery sooner rather than later is important to you, don't buy furniture at stores that sell custom pieces, or you'll be waiting forever! Amazingly, the Williams-Sonoma Home catalogue now boasts that it offers delivery of upholstered pieces in forty-five days, and some other retailers offer delivery within six weeks or less. Keep in mind, though, that even when a retailer gives you an approximate delivery date, many unpredictable variables may still come into play—labor and transportation strikes, shipping glitches, or a host of other unforeseen events. When it comes to furniture delivery, it's best not to expect immediate gratification, or you might be disappointed.

Antiques vs. reproductions: Buy what you like!
Many friends have asked me over the years whether they should feel obligated to buy antiques—the "real

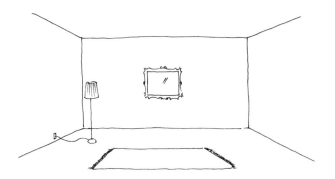

thing"—instead of reproductions. In many cases, people are swayed by the convincing arguments of antiques dealers, who contend that antiques will hold their value, but reproductions won't.

When it comes to antiques and reproductions, it's important to understand that *both are fine*. Different pieces appeal to different people, and the result is that you should buy only what you like. A friend once told me that a house filled with antiques would make her feel more like she was living in a surreal page from *House Beautiful* than a woman with a busy life and four children. In her case, antiques are not always practical. But it truly depends on the situation.

Today, many reproductions have come a long way from the sometimes poor construction and weak resemblance to the originals that characterized such pieces years ago. In addition, many of today's reproduction pieces are made with a greater understanding for how contemporary society lives. As a result, there are all kinds of new bells and whistles built into the more recently constructed reproductions that are attractive to today's homeowners, such as greater durability, more resilient, easy-to-care-for finishes, and added storage features. Baker is one company

that has lived up to an excellent reputation in the re-production world.

I do want to say, though, that not all antiques are rickety or overly fragile. Such pieces can also be highly functional and very solid—sometimes, as in the case of pieces made from 19th-century woods, they can even be far sturdier than pieces built today. Also, always remember that the value of antiques can fluctuate with the economy and the public's ever-changing taste. The decision to buy reproductions or antiques should thus be a purely subjective decision based on your own personal taste.

Get rid of that musty antique smell! Years ago, I inherited my grandmother's dining room table. I loved the table, but the musty smell was driving me crazy. I feared that for the rest of my life I would be forced to live with that terrible smell, and so would my dinner guests.

Thankfully, this doesn't have to be a lifelong problem. Through the years, I've discovered that the best way to get rid of that musty smell in older pieces like grandma's dining table is to have them thoroughly cleaned and waxed. You can actually hire someone to come to your house to do this professionally—in fact, I suggest having a professional do this once a year

because it will not only help keep the musty smell at bay, but will also keep the wood looking and feeling great to the touch. Call me crazy, but I happen to love the smell of freshly waxed furniture. In fact, in one furniture store I reviewed positively in my first book, *Furniture Hot Spots*, I remember the first thing that hit me when I walked into the shop was the clean scent of the recently waxed furniture in its showroom! Another option if you don't mind your wood getting a little faded is to put it outside for a day and let it air out. And watch out: I've found that putting cedar blocks in furniture makes the smell worse instead of better!

Don't be afraid to buy at auction. A client of mine once confided to me that she felt more comfortable and more in control when buying furniture in a regular store than she did when buying at auction. She said that she once went to an auction and panicked when it was time to sit in the audience and bid against other audience members—it felt, she said, like all eyes were on her when she raised her paddle.

The truth is that you may actually have more control over the final price of a piece when you buy it at auction. That being said, however, it's still important to do your homework. Years ago when my husband and I went to our first auction, we mistakenly thought we were big winners because we succeeded in buying everything we wanted. Sadly, we later realized that we had overpaid for everything. Our fiasco taught me that, when bidding on furniture at an auction, it's best to research the pieces on which you'll be bidding and set a strict monetary cap that you will not exceed. Once you set sound limits for yourself, you can

REDFLAG*

Think Before You Shop—What to Remember When Buying Furniture:

> Find out where your potential interior designer buys furniture for his clients.

> Ask for a closed-end contract from your interior designer. Set a cap on the hours that can be billed or the commission that can be charged for each purchase.

> When buying an antique, ask the dealer to provide a certificate of authenticity.

> To ensure a piece's authenticity, ask the dealer to prove to you how he knows its genre.

> Antiques are not necessarily better investments than reproductions or contemporary pieces.

> It is possible to remove the musty smell of antiques through cleaning and waxing.

> Auctions are a good place to start when buying furniture for your home.

> Ask what shipping charges will be added to your furniture purchase.

> Ask for a written warranty when buying new furniture.

take comfort knowing that you have control over the bidding process. Remember: though there are great bargains to be had at auctions, there is no set rule about what type of venue is least expensive for buyers. The final price at an auction will depend on many factors—the weather (which greatly affects buyer turnout), the time of day the auction is held, demand for that particular style of furniture, location, and the negotiating ability of others participating in the bidding process. So don't be afraid, but do be prepared!

2

Selecting Furniture

Critical Pointers
to Make You
Savvy, Not Sorry

For years, people have been asking me how they can determine whether they are paying the right price for the furniture they want. No expert, including myself, can always know the "right" price of a piece—if there even is such a thing. Why? Because pricing is not a science. There are, however, several factors you should be aware of that can help you better determine what price you should pay for furniture.

When buying furniture, I advise drawing from the old cliché, "Beauty is only skin deep." Never make the mistake of basing a buying decision solely on the looks or style of a piece; no matter how extraordinary the piece, you must explore beyond its aesthetics and examine its construction. This philosophy especially applies to the two most basic kinds of furniture we buy: upholstered goods and case goods. Upholstered goods include couches, chairs, and other kinds of seating with attached fabric. Case goods are generally made from wood. According to a recent survey conducted by the American Home Furnishings Alliance (AHFA), 22 percent of all people are likely to make furniture-buying mistakes when purchasing a sofa. To avoid becoming one of those unhappy campers in the 22nd percentile, before you make your next sofa choice you must look beyond the obvious features, such as exquisite fabrics or great comfort. To know if the piece is well-designed from the inside out, you will need to know something about its internal parts, as well as some of its other construction properties.

When I was running my retail furniture store, many people confided to me that they had no clue how furniture is actually put together—let alone what specific features they needed to look for to determine whether a piece was well-made, using quality standards. This alarming lack of knowledge on the part of the furniture consumer is more widespread than you might suppose. A recent study conducted by the San Francisco Design Center found that most Americans in the market for furniture say that even with all of the furniture shopping options available today—larger chain stores, convenient online shopping, auctions, catalogs, etc.—they still place the majority of their trust in their local retail furniture stores to help them make sound buying decisions. But relying heavily on a local retailer to help you select the upholstered piece of furniture that's right for you is not the best idea. In fact, when it comes to making furniture-buying decisions, relying on *anyone* besides yourself is not a wise strategy! While there are many veteran retail salespeople with great integrity who will work hard to help you make the right choice that is solely to your benefit—I know you're out there and I'm so grateful!—there are also those in the sales force who are paid on a commission basis. The more these salespeople sell, the more money they make for themselves—and because of this conflict of interest, they'll lure you to a higher-priced piece every time, simply because it generates a nice commission for them to pocket!

In order to choose the upholstered piece that's best for you, you will have to become more knowledgeable about its construction. But don't fret! You can accomplish this without giving up your career and taking on an assembly line job at a furniture factory. There are a few simple and specific things you can do that will make a big difference in helping you become a smart shopper of upholstered goods. In this chapter, I'll pass along some tips for you to use when considering which upholstered or wood pieces to buy. In addition, I have called upon experienced retail experts from major players in the retail industry to share their expert advice on buying these kinds of pieces.

Selecting Upholstered Furniture

Most shoppers become perplexed when shopping for upholstered pieces because there are so many styles, fabrics, fillings, and price ranges from which to choose. But understanding the overall quality of an upholstered piece really just comes down to understanding its most basic components: the frame, springs, cushions, and fabric.

Frames: The Bones of a Piece

Most of us will never see an exposed frame in an upholstered piece, so we tend to forget that such a thing even exists under all that beautiful fabric and soft cushioning. But I can't tell you how many people have E-mailed me over the years with stories about how they learned this lesson the hard way—how they were besotted with a gorgeous chair or couch, only to have their dreams crushed when their dream piece literally began to fall apart after they brought it home.

The first thing you need to do when you spot a piece that interests you is to ask the salesperson what kinds of materials were used to make the frame. Until recently, the best frames were made from kiln-dried hardwood. Examples of this kind of hardwood include oak, maple, birch, and alder. With kiln-dried hardwoods and other woods, it is critical that the wood used for the frame be dry in order to resist warping or weakening. Also, the harder the wood, the more likely it will be that the hardware in the piece will stay in place and not fall apart. Although kiln-dried wood has been the material of choice for upholstered pieces for hundreds of years, today's frames are also made from many good alternatives that will stand the test of time equally well. Steel, hardwood, and softwood plywood are all examples of commonly used materials that make for extremely strong frames.

In addition to finding out which materials make up the frame, you must also determine if the frame is well constructed. To determine this, you'll need to be somewhat hands-on and give the piece what I call a good "test run." In many ways, testing out an upholstered piece is a little like buying a used automobile. Before buying a car, you test-drive it. You might also open the hood and take a good look inside. And there are those among us who even kick the tires—though I wouldn't suggest trying the latter on a couch, unless you enjoy being confronted by a large person in a uniform wearing a badge! When buying furniture, a thorough "test run" is similarly important. In particular, when it comes to upholstered pieces you must not be shy about asking if you can "open the hood" to check for staples. Staples are not a good way to reinforce joints in an upholstered piece—in lieu of them, glue and proper reinforcement hardware should be attached to the critical joints.

I once tested dozens of sofas in order to select the *Consumers Digest* "Best Buy" in the sleeper sofa category. After crawling around an entire showroom filled with couches, prodding and poking as well as flipping over a number of pillows and cushions, I was absolutely amazed at the poor quality I discovered in the construction of the sleepers in many of the big chain stores—even the ones that were made by famous furniture manufacturers. But perhaps just as discouraging to me was the lack of shopping savvy on the part of the other shoppers who were looking at the same sofas. Most of them seemed totally in the dark about what they should be looking for—they were far too passive about checking out the pieces, often simply sitting on them timidly before making up their minds. I, on the other hand, knew the importance of taking off the cushions and inspecting below the mattress of each piece. When I did so, I often saw exposed, raw plywood with a bunch of sloppy-looking staples all over the frame. Not only should the plywood never have been exposed in this way, but these sofas should never have been finished using staples in the first place. Those poor, unsuspecting shoppers! I decided I needed to help them out, because the salespeople would never have alerted them to the poor quality of the frames in the pieces they were buying—not that salespeople always know the difference!

When it comes to frames, there is one more critical rule that you should observe: Check to see that the corners are reinforced using blocks. Blocks are simple rectangular pieces that are glued onto the frame of a sofa at stress points, usually at the corners. Sometimes it is possible to see them, sometimes not. If you don't see blocks, ask your salesperson if they are there. Don't ever underestimate blocks; they are very important because they lend additional support and ensure that the piece will remain stable and strong. And don't be self-conscious about getting down on the showroom floor and stealing a peek underneath a couch to see if it has blocks. As further insurance that the piece has sufficient support, I even recommend that you "kick the tires" a bit by shaking the couch lightly. If blocks are positioned at the proper stress points, they will reinforce the piece and prevent it from wobbling.

Springs: A Spring by Any Other Name?

Springs can be confusing. We often hear salespeople talking about different types of coils and spring counts in couches and mattresses, and most of us feel like we are listening to a lecture on anatomy. Compounding the confusion today because of improved technology, more manufacturers are using steel springs for durability. For the sake of simplicity, however, the main thing you need to keep in mind is that the greater the spring count of a mattress, the better the support and comfort it will provide.

But does the type of spring really matter? To answer this question, I decided to call upon veterans from the sales forces of several major players in the retail furniture industry and ask them to clear up the relationship between man-made springs and machine-made springs. I also asked them to clarify how the type of springs used can affect the price of a piece. As it turns out, when it comes to springs, the old saying "you get what you pay for" turns out to be true. In fact, veteran retail sales consultants at Ethan Allen, Thomasville, Bloomingdale's, Furnitureland South in High Point, North Carolina, and Marshall Field's—an old and highly respected retail source in Chicago—unanimously concurred that hand-tied springs lend far better quality to a piece than machine-made springs.

The experts agreed that, although machine-made steel springs are less expensive to manufacture and may ultimately result in a less expensive couch, hand-tied springs are more apt to stay in place. They also agreed that the best-quality coils are often hand-tied with twine in several knots. So while you can expect to pay a higher price for a couch with a high spring count or springs that are handmade, you'll get a higher-quality piece that will probably give you many years of good wear.

Cushions: The "Flesh" of a Piece

Cushion filling has become an industry of its own; today it seems that there are countless kinds of fillings from which to choose. Many of you may be familiar with foam as a common stuffing for cushions. But although foam is the most common material used for upholstered goods, many other kinds of materials can also be used—including down, polyester fiber, and cotton—and one isn't necessarily better than the other.

Today, many manufacturers are engineering cushions that are fire resistant. Some newly improved kinds of foam materials are flame resistant, which may become the standard in the upholstery business if major governmental watchdogs and consumer advocates get their way.

Another important feature of foam is its density: the denser the foam, the stronger the cushion. According to the American Home Furnishings Association, "the best quality upholstered furniture uses a density rating of 1.8 to 2.5." Aside from durability, density also makes for a much more comfortable piece. In general, the greater its density, the more a cushion conforms to you and cushions your movements. But along with all this density, there of course comes a higher price tag.

As a contributing writer for *Consumers Digest*, one of my assignments was to select the best sleeper sofa and futon on the market at that time, and I spent an incredible amount of time testing and researching hundreds of these products in dozens of stores. After a while, however, I felt just like I do when I shop for perfume: all of the pieces started to seem alike, and I couldn't tell any of them apart! The same may hold true for you when you are shopping for a couch or chair. Although you will hopefully never be faced with the task of having to try out as many couches as I did for my writing assignment, I still wouldn't recommend trying out one right after the other, because they may all start to feel the same.

The best way to get a good feel for a couch is to sit in it without adding extra throw pillows. Such pillows will give a false sense of security, and once they are removed the couch will feel completely different. Remember: The couch you choose is a piece you will have to live with every day, and you should feel entitled to get to know it well before bringing it home. I also encourage you, as strange as it may look to others, to lounge on the couch in the store in the

REDFLAG*

The Nuts and Bolts of Cushions and Frames—What to Remember When Buying Upholstered Pieces:

> Check frame construction to make sure the joinery is strong—no staples!

> Look for kiln-dried hardwood, steel, or hardwood and softwood plywood frames.

> Make sure there is no exposed plywood inside the sofa.

> Check to make sure blocks are used for added reinforcement.

> Ask about spring count—higher is better.

> Hand-tied springs are better than machine-made.

> The denser the foam, the more durable the cushion.

same way you might at home. Being able to kick back and relax on a couch in the store, just as you would do on your favorite couch at home, will help you choose a piece that will provide you with many years of comfort.

Fabric Covers: The Virtues of Synthetics

While natural fabrics like linen, cotton, wool, and silk will never go out of style, I am finding many wonderful synthetic fabrics are also extremely popular—not only because they are attractive, but also because they are incredibly durable and virtually stainproof. Tightly woven fabrics, seen both in synthetics and natural materials, generally wear better than looser fabrics because they are stronger.

The virtues of the new synthetic fabrics were recently driven home for me on a shopping trip to Boston. I visited a store called Shoominè, which featured a large, luscious red couch—a piece so inviting that when I plopped myself down on it, I immediately felt as though I was being wrapped in a cozy blanket. The store owner told me all about the soft yet durable fabric from which it was made—a unique cotton chenille, made in Germany and mixed with some miraculous kind of stain-resistant Teflon that is also environmentally friendly. Before this fabric leaves the factory, I learned, it must undergo a battery of tests—tests to see whether it fades in direct sunlight, pilling tests, laundering tests to see how it holds up in the washing machine, and even a test in which a special machine rubs the fabric 25,000 times to see how it wears! I was also pleasantly surprised to learn that the fabric came with a five-year manufacturer's warranty. Moreover, the owner informed me that buyers could use soap and water right on the surface of the fabric, rather than having to fit entire slipcovers in the washing machine. Finally, to demonstrate the fabric's stain resistance, the store owner actually poured coffee on the couch to prove that it would not penetrate into the fabric. Sure enough, no stain!

In my opinion, the new technologies used to make upholstery fabrics have covered all the bases. I would never hesitate to buy these new fabrics or any pieces made from them.

Leather: Handle with Care

A short time ago, I received an E-mail from a woman named Bonnie asking me if she could dye her leather couch a different color. I told her that dying leather might ruin the material, and did not recommend that she attempt it. As leather couches have increased in popularity over the past few years due to lowered prices, consumers are striving to better understand the characteristics of this material and how to care for their leather pieces.

There are many types of leather and dyes. Leather comes from an animal hide that has undergone a tanning, or preservation, process. The top portion of a hide—the layer just under the fur—yields a much stronger and more durable skin, and is referred to as "top grain." The softer, weaker leathers—such as suede—are called "bottom grain" and come from the deeper layers of the hide. Both Nubuck and suede are buffed to be soft, but Nubuck is stronger and more durable leather than suede, which tends to show more wear and tear. Suede is also usually less expensive than Nubuck. The softer a leather feels, the weaker it usually is, and the more likely it is to fall apart over time.

Today's dyes cover most imperfections or discolorations in leather, but need to be carefully applied. To preserve the color of the dye, keep the leather out of direct sunlight and keep it clean and dust-free. And while we're on the subject of dust, if you're someone who dislikes dusting furniture regularly, a roomful of leather furniture may not be for you—keeping your leather dust-free is important for its preservation, but is also a lot of work. I recently called on Leather Solutions, a leather furniture repair shop out of Long Island, New York (contact them by phone at 516-223-3340), to consult with one of the country's greatest leather experts, Richard Daly, about the issue of dust. According to Daly, one of the most common problems with leather is the soil that is attracted by dust particles—soil that will eventually penetrate into the leather and become difficult to remove. Daly advises that the best method for getting

REDFLAG*

Hide and Seek—What to Remember When Buying Leather:

> The top portion of the hide—called the "top grain"—is the most durable.

> Softer leathers come from the bottom grains of a hide.

> Nubuck is generally stronger and more expensive than suede.

> Keep leather out of the sun, and keep it clean and dust-free.

> Clean leather with dishwashing soap, warm water, and a sponge.

rid of this soil is to mix dishwasher detergent into a pan of water until the mixture turns sudsy. Once the water is sudsy, gather only the suds (and *not* the water) on a soft, damp sponge, and gently wipe the leather. Then wipe the piece with a separate clean damp cloth to remove all soapy residues.

Stains on leather are also problematic, and are especially difficult to remove because liquid absorbs quickly into leather. So the next time your accident-prone friend drops by for dinner and topples his refreshment onto your leather sofa, you need to take quick action. In order to avoid any kind of permanent damage, tend to the stain immediately with a damp—*not* soaking wet—sponge to blot out the stain.

So far, leather sounds like a lot of work—and it is. But I do want to mention something in its favor: its remarkable tendency to change color over time. Unlike other coverings, leather tends to look better the more wear it gets.

Flammability and Fabric: Think Safety

The Upholstered Furniture Action Council (UFAC) has created voluntary fire safety standards that manufacturers of fabric often follow. A gold UFAC tag will let you know that a fabric was made using these important safety guidelines.

Selecting Case Goods: To Cherish or Not to Cherish?

Case goods are chests, tables, chairs, cabinetry, or other non-upholstered pieces that are made from wood. Some of the most cherished and treasured pieces in our homes, such as dining tables or desks, often fall into this category. In fact, many consumers assume that when they buy case goods made from solid wood, they are purchasing the kind of quality pieces that they will cherish as future heirlooms—after all, "solid wood furniture" is synonymous with "quality." Or is it?

A couple of months ago, I received an E-mail from a woman named Joan asking me how to tell if a piece was made from solid wood. She said that on several occasions while shopping for furniture, she had been misled by overzealous salespeople who insisted that their inventories were made from solid wood when in fact they were not. The allegedly solid-wood furniture she purchased had begun falling apart, in part because it was actually made from processed wood materials—not solid wood at all. Joan's query about how to identify solid-wood furniture is thus an important one, because not all pieces made from wood are created equal.

There are two main types of wood from which we make our furniture. One is hardwood, which includes mahogany, maple, birch, oak, cherry, and walnut, among others. The second is softwood, which includes pine, spruce, fir, and redwood. Don't make the mistake of assuming that just because a piece is made from softwood, it is necessarily less durable than one made from hardwood. In reference to wood, the terms "hard" and "soft" refer only to whether the tree from which the wood is taken loses its leaves seasonally—as in the case of hardwood—or keeps them all year long, as in the case of softwood.

It is possible that several different kinds of woods can be used in the construction of a single piece of furniture. For example, the term "solid walnut armoire" indicates that all of the armoire's visible exterior parts are constructed of solid wood. However, other parts in the armoire's interior might be made of another type of wood, or even a combination of other woods. Using a combination of woods to make a piece is acceptable, so long as the piece is strong and its materials are described accurately to the customer. I firmly believe that, in furniture stores, there should be a label attached to each piece telling you its exact wood composition. This description should be accurate and easy to understand, just like with food labels.

Types of Woods

Solid Wood. Solid wood is often used for carved pieces, legs, and stretchers (the part that connects the legs of a piece). In order for solid wood to be considered strong and durable, it needs to be cut along the grain when dry. Cross-grain designs—those cut against the grain—are considered weaker than solid-wood designs. It is easier to carve wood that is solid, because the wood can support finer details.

Plywood. Most furniture today is made with some plywood. Plywood is made by gluing together multiple thin layers of wood. It is sometimes even stronger than solid wood because of all the layering involved. Plywood can also be bent and shaped more easily than solid wood. You can purchase plywood in various thicknesses. As I discuss in greater detail at the end of this chapter—see the section on organic furniture—some of the chemicals used in bonding plywood are controversial, and many in the scientific community believe that these chemicals can pose serious health dangers to consumers.

Particle Board. I sometimes think of particle board as "the other wood"—a reference to those TV commercials advertising pork as the "other white meat." Particle board is made from wood dust, chips, and flakes that are combined with various resins and adhesives. It is an easy wood to use if you want to create a certain shape, or form. Because particle board has no graining like solid wood, it will not warp or split. Environmentalists, however, are very critical of this material and suspect that, like plywood, it is made from similar components that can cause an array of health problems.

Veneers. Usually made from more expensive or rare wood, a veneer covers the surface of a piece of furniture. In the Victorian days, many veneers were mass-produced and manufactured with inferior woods. Some of the better veneers are made with burl—a darker-colored wood, prized for its beauty, that is taken from a malformation in a tree—or unusual kinds of mahogany that feature an extraordinary grain. Veneers come in many thicknesses. Because of their fine quality, veneers are harder to work with than other kinds of woods because they need to stay thin. Veneers come in small sheets, so the sheets need to be carefully matched to show the same grain and color. Chippen-

REDFLAG[*]

Preparing for a Grainy Day—What to Remember About Buying Woods:

> Hardwoods are not necessarily more durable than softwoods.

> When carving designs, solid wood is easier to work with than woods cut across the grain.

> Plywood is made from many thin layers of wood.

> Made from a combination of materials, particle board is good for forming shapes.

dale and Hepplewhite, the 18th-century English cabinetmakers, were known for their master craftsmanship when it came to veneered furniture.

Joinery

The term "joinery" refers to the way in which pieces of wood are connected to create a strong piece of furniture. Modern technology has brought us a long way from the time of the ancient Egyptian dynasties, when joints were secured with simple leather thongs. Today dovetails, screws, and mortises and tenons are often used to secure the best-made wooden case goods. Wood blocks are also used to reinforce the strength of joints, and glue is often applied to joints to lend even greater security in keeping the pieces attached. As I mentioned in the upholstery section, stay away from staples. Staples and nails are shoddy ways to secure a piece of furniture, because they can become loose and fall out over time. Use of nails and staples not only signals that a piece is of inferior quality, but also can pose a serious hazard to small children and pets.

Understanding joinery will not only tell you how well a piece was constructed, but will also give you an idea about pricing and whether you may be overpaying for a poorly made piece. Stability is the most important element of furniture. When inspecting a piece, don't just look at the outside. You need to ex-

REDFLAG*

Keeping It All Together—What to Remember About Joinery:

> Dovetailing, screws, wood blocks, mortise and tenon are often used to secure the best made wood case goods.

> Stay away from staples!

amine the overall joinery so you don't make the wrong buying decision. Open up the drawers and make sure they feel strong. Slide them in and out several times to make sure they glide smoothly and that they are a good fit for the piece. Gently run your fingers across the bottom of the inside of the drawers to make sure they are well sanded and finished smoothly. Always check out the knobs; try to jiggle them to make sure they are not wobbly. And remember: hinges need to be strong enough for the piece they are trying to support.

Finishes

I can't tell you how many times people ask me what the right way is to finish furniture. While I believe different kinds of wood and different pieces should be finished differently, there are some basic guidelines. Recently, while reviewing a furniture store that sold 19th-century furniture from Indonesia, I immediately noticed something strange about the way its pieces appeared to have been finished improperly. Instead of looking and feeling like the well-crafted, naturally weathered, rustic wooden pieces of 19th-century Indonesia, the pieces appeared scratchy, as though improperly sanded, with an inauthentic

REDFLAG[✳]

Finish Strong—What to Remember About Finishes:

> A well-finished piece emphasizes the beauty of the piece's own grain and has a natural appearance.

> Due to the layering of paint, lacquered finishes chip and show scratches easily.

> Finishes properly applied should absorb into the piece.

> Period furniture should be finished in a manner appropriate to its period.

glossy-looking shine. I take finishes very seriously—after all, a poor finish can cause the value of a piece to decrease—and knowing that these pieces were not properly finished caused me immediately to lower my rating for the store.

While I believe that different pieces made from different kinds of wood can and should be finished differently, there are, nonetheless, some basic guidelines that apply to all pieces. Well-constructed wood furniture should be made with a finish that emphasizes the wood's own natural beauty and grain. Some finishes are simply applied to the top of a piece of wood, but do not penetrate—these kinds of finishes are not as desirable as those that are absorbed into the wood. A finish that is applied by hand-rubbing is considered the best. And finally, although high-gloss finishes, and even lacquer, can make a piece look special, such finishes are harder to maintain and show more scratches.

Organic Furniture: Now You Can Eat Your Organic Peach on Your Organic Couch

I know a woman who suffers from bad asthma. She was told by her doctor to try to eliminate some of the chemicals present in her home, from those found in detergents and cleaning products to those found in her furniture. Previously unaware that her furniture could contain harmful chemicals, she called me to ask what I knew about so-called "organic furniture." Organic furniture has been popular in Europe for many years, but little is known about it here in America. As the world goes organic in everything from food to clothing, and now even in its furniture, we should understand what the benefits are of organic furniture. Is organic furniture really necessary for safeguarding our health and environment? Or is it just another fad or gimmick?

To answer these questions, I called upon Jesse Johnson—an expert on organic furniture and co-owner of the store Q Collection in New York, where he carries some of the most beautiful organic furniture I have ever seen—to describe the basic functions of organic furniture and the materials from which it is made. According to Johnson, the goal of organic-furniture production by his and other companies is to "eliminate toxic chemicals, carcinogens and the leading components of poor indoor air quality." Johnson, and the industry in general, strive for the following benefits through production of their "sustainable" products:

- Reduction of temperature changes and acid rain
- Improvement of air quality, both indoors and out-doors

REDFLAG*

Saving the Planet Begins at Home—Organic Solutions for Furniture Construction:

While the science of perfecting organic furniture is evolving, there are simple steps furniture manufacturers can take to improve the environmental friendliness of their operations:

> Use vegetable dyes when dying fabric and leather.

> Protect our natural environment by only using woods that have been certified for organic use by the Forest Stewardship Council (FSC), an organization that approves the management of certain forests.

> Eliminate the use of toxic materials like formaldehyde, polyurethane, and particle board, in addition to pesticides, fertilizers, and flame retardants.

- Conservation of water and improvement of water quality
- Waste reduction and facilitation of the ability to reuse and recycle
- Conservation of energy
- Improvement of human health
- Preservation of habitat

Formaldehyde and polyurethane, two common carcinogenic materials, are regularly used in non-organic furniture production. Formaldehyde is a component of many adhesives, particularly those used in construction of furniture from pressed board and plywood. Formaldehyde not only pollutes the air, but can also cause upper-respiratory infections and asthma, and the World Health Organization has declared that it is known to cause cancer in humans. Found in foam products, polyurethane is also known to cause cancer in humans, and long-term exposure is known to cause lung problems. Elimination of these harmful chemicals—and those like them—from the manufacturing process is one of the main goals of organic furniture production.

Selecting Furniture that Fits Your Lifestyle

In this chapter we have discussed many aspects of furniture shopping that you need to consider before making your next purchase. We've covered some basics about how quality furniture should be constructed. We have also learned the importance of taking a hands-on role in examining furniture—specifically, we have seen how turning over cushions, a little jiggling here and there, and using our sense of touch all play a major role in the shopping process.

There is, however, one last factor to be considered in the difficult process of furniture shopping—and that is lifestyle.

I cannot stress enough the importance of considering your family's personality and lifestyle when choosing furniture that is truly right for you. Determining the authenticity of an antique, or even choosing the piece with the best quality, is only one part of the big picture. When choosing your furniture, always keep in mind that while the pieces we choose are only made of fabric and wood, not flesh and bone, they are far more than just sedentary parts of our lives. Furniture plays a very real and active role in our everyday lives—it is an integral part of the space in which we live, work, play, and grow. So make sure that your next furniture purchase will serve your needs well—and that it will bring comfort, joy, and warmth into the lives of you and your family.

Final Thoughts on Buying Furniture

With all the options we have today for buying furniture, there are some basic guidelines we want to follow for making wise purchases.

When buying upholstered furniture, remember to ask the salesperson about the composition of the couch—from the frame, to the cushion filling, to the fabric. Ask about the springs: how many and what kind? Remember to look for a denser filling, and don't forget to ask about the properties of the material being used for the upholstery. When selecting fabrics, don't forget to ask how to clean them—and if they are slip covers, make sure they will actually fit into your washing machine. Make sure that the fabrics won't fade or pill.

With case goods, ask the retailer to tell you the kind of woods used to make the furniture. If there are veneers, find out what kinds of wood were used to make them. Remember to ask about the joinery, and check to make sure the piece is stable. And look for wood glides on drawers and dust covers between drawers for added strength.

Organic furniture is becoming more and more popular in the U.S. Made without the use of harsh chemicals that can damage our bodies and the environment, organic furniture not only helps to prevent asthma and allergy attacks on the part of its buyers, it also contributes to a movement toward environmental friendliness on the part of the furniture-making industry.

Informing yourself about each of these elements in the furniture-buying process will help you make smarter choices on your next shopping adventure.

3

Raising Your Antiques IQ

Clues that Spell
"F-A-K-E"

hen it comes to furniture, many people only want to buy the "real thing," and want nothing to do with reproductions. They feel that reproductions won't hold their value as well as antiques, or they associate reproductions with inferior quality. Many reproductions look like obvious fakes, but there are also many good reproductions that closely resemble authentic period pieces. Knowing the "real thing" when you see it is an important part of shopping for furniture.

If you are considering buying an antique, you should be aware of some important features that will indicate whether a piece is authentic—that is, from the period its seller represents. In this chapter, I'll discuss what you should look out for when shopping for an authentic piece.

Right Period, Wrong Wood

As I discussed in Chapter Two, you need to know what type of wood is appropriate for the piece that you are buying. Especially when shopping for antiques, it is important to know what types of woods were used during the period in which a particular piece was made. For example, if you were considering buying what you believed to be a pair of English Regency chairs and the dealer told you the chairs were made from pine, you would need to know that pine was not used to make Regency chairs—and that the chairs must thus be reproductions.

Knowing your woods will thus allow you to tell reproductions from authentic antiques. For example, a reproduction of a piece originally made in the 1700s could have been made in the late 1800s, so it will still look old—just not as old as an original piece. Knowing your woods will allow you to tell the difference. Many of the woods used to make furniture before 1900 were native to the countries in which the furniture was constructed. These woods were used because they were easy to acquire, and craftsmen could make greater quantities of furniture without needing to travel to find wood.

Many years ago, my husband wanted to buy a chess table that we found in France. The dealer trying to sell us the table told us all kinds of stories about the piece—it was from 1926, he claimed, and it came from the home of the former governor of French Vietnam. He then produced a slew of details to support his claims. In these types of situations, when dealers are bombarding you with information, be careful. Don't listen to all of the dealers' stories regarding provenance, because you may get caught up in the moment. Instead, remember your woods. We ended up buying this chess table—not because of the dealer's charming stories, but because the kinds of woods used in the piece (pallisander, ebony, and walnut) indicated to us that the piece was authentic. Easy!

Right Furniture, Wrong Finish

Years ago, I met a woman who was shopping for a kitchen table. She wanted a large pine table (pine was all the rage back then), and asked if she could show me one that she was considering purchasing from a so-called "pine antiques store." (By the way, much of what is labeled "antique pine furniture" is really just old barn wood that has been cobbled together piecemeal to create a piece of furniture.) I agreed to go shopping with her. When I got to the store, I noticed that the table was not an original farm table. It had new legs and looked as if it had been coated at least fifty times with shiny polyurethane—something you'd never see on the real thing! While this sort of coating can help prevent food and other particles from lodging in between the cracks of a piece, in general it is a very difficult surface to maintain over time. The finish must match the style and period. I encouraged this woman to find a truly old farm table, which she could easily find for no more money than this hodgepodge.

Right Piece, Wrong Façade or Hardware

While reviewing stores for my last book, *Furniture Hot Spots*, I reviewed a well-known antiques store in a large city. I had heard so many wonderful things about its unusual inventory that I was excited over the prospect of paying it a visit. While browsing the store, however, I was shocked to observe that the woman who owned the store had covered an early-19th-century English chest in plaid wool fabric. When I asked why she had covered up the piece, she told me that she had wanted to give the chest a fresh, updated look.

The lesson of this story is an important one: If you're thinking about buying a covered piece, find out what's underneath the fabric before agreeing to pay some outrageous price for what may very well be a remake in disguise. Remember, an antique will only hold its value if it hasn't been materially changed.

You should also notice if a piece's hardware has been changed. While hardware alone won't affect the sale value of an antique, a change in its hardware is often an indicator of its authenticity. Changed hardware is often a red flag, indicating that the piece has been changed in some other major way, or perhaps even that the piece is nothing more than a fake strung together with parts from various other pieces.

Right Piece, Wrong Upholstery or Paint Finish

Years ago I went to an auction and bought a beautiful Scandinavian bench from the 1800s. Despite the fact it was painted an awful shade of green, I couldn't pass it up because it had such graceful lines and the price was so low. I really didn't know much about the piece, and the local auction house couldn't provide me with many details, so I asked an antiques restorer—also known as a conservationist—to come

REDFLAG*

Buyer Beware!—What to Remember When Shopping for Antiques:

> Make sure a piece is made from wood that is appropriate for its period.

> Don't rely on a dealer's stories when determining whether a piece is authentic—do your own research!

> Make sure a piece's finish is representative of furniture from that period.

> Examine a piece's hardware to make sure it matches hardware from furniture of that period. Replaced hardware won't necessarily lower the value of the piece, but it may indicate that other material changes have been made.

> Make sure excessive paint isn't covering up some major defect—it is very difficult to strip or melt paint.

> An upholstered piece is usually more valuable with its original fabric.

and take a look at it. When I asked him what we could do to go back to the piece's original paint, he said that the process would be extremely complicated—we would have to melt down each layer of paint carefully in order to get to the original layer. In the end, the piece proved to be more trouble than it was worth, since the repainting had significantly lowered its value.

The bottom line is this: Touching up or repainting an antique can lower its value, not to mention make it look odd. The same goes for reupholstering. I love old chairs—especially when they feature original fabric, because replacing original antique upholstery can be treacherous. Today, even if an old upholstered piece has an uncomfortable seat, advanced upholstering technologies can be used to reupholster the piece using its original fabric—provided that such fabric is intact.

4

Mission Impossible

Decoding
Furniture Prices

While researching my book, *Furniture Hot Spots*, I shopped incognito at more than 500 furniture stores nationwide. Along the way, I noticed what seemed like an army of perplexed customers with blank stares on their faces, all facing showrooms of couches and dressers that seemed identical in every way except for price. I watched countless shoppers examining furniture tags as though they were trying to figure out riddles on the backs of cereal boxes—rereading them over and over, hoping to discover some hidden clue they had overlooked that would tell them why some pieces of furniture were priced higher than seemingly comparable pieces displayed nearby.

Actually, the average shopper's uncertainty—the confusion that arises from considering the differences, if any, between a $1,000 couch or dresser and a $5,000 couch or dresser—doesn't surprise me in the least. Why? Because the retail industry and furniture stores, in particular, are not focused on educating the consumer. Furniture stores have one main objective: to sell furniture, and to motivate buyers to "buy up"—that is, to buy more expensive pieces than they originally intend—even at the expense of facilitating informed consumer decisions. Consider, for example, those furniture tags that I witness shoppers obsessing over. These tags describe merchandise in only the vaguest terms; the construction techniques and materials used to make a piece often are not listed, or are listed incorrectly, and in many cases are not known even to the dealer. Compounding this problem is the fact that many customers are simply too embarrassed to ask a salesperson for more information—about the differences, for example, between a more popular brand-name piece and its clone-like, cheaper alternative.

So how can you avoid being just another clueless shopper when it comes to recognizing basic differences in furniture quality? By reading this chapter, you'll learn the fundamentals of furniture pricing, and you'll learn what to look for when you're reading a tag, examining a label, or talking to a sales associate. To help bring you this information, I decided to go undercover in the world of furniture retail. My real-life "mission impossible" was to find out once and for all what differentiates a $1,000 couch or dresser from a $5,000 version of the same piece. I brought our questions about price differences and quality directly to the most experienced "super" professional, veteran salespeople in the retail industry. The retail stores I chose to investigate on my mission were some of the best-known furniture retailers in the country: Thomasville, Ethan Allen, Bloomingdale's, Marshall Field's, and Furnitureland South—retailers that serve a variety of geographic areas and socioeconomic groups, and that are known for their high levels of service and quality. Their answers to my questions are presented in this chapter.

Truth or Dare: Putting Furniture Stores to the Test

In researching this book, I visited dozens of retail stores incognito and worked with dozens of salespeople, allowing each to help me make smart choices when selecting the best couches and dressers for my money. I told each salesperson that I was able to spend no more than $1,000 on a couch, and asked him or her to point out the best couch I could purchase within my budget. I also asked each salesperson to tell me the qualitative difference between a $1,000 couch and a $5,000 couch. I then repeated the same exercise with dressers. What follows is a synopsis of the answers I received.

A Good $1,000 Couch: Is It Possible?

Most retailers informed me that they definitely offered some good-quality couches for roughly $1,000. As for differences in quality between expensive and inexpensive pieces, a salesman named Andy at Thomasville—who had been selling furniture for quite a few years and whom I thought seemed very knowledgeable and honest—claimed that the difference in quality between a $1,000 couch and a $5,000 couch would *not* be as significant as some might think. The real differences between the two price tags, he claimed, would be the sizes of the sofas and the available fabric choices: generally speaking, the more expensive the couch, the larger it will be and more fabric upgrades will be available.

As it turned out, the majority of salespeople from our retail stores seemed to unanimously agree with Andy—that fabric quality and size are two factors that weigh heavily in determining price differences between couches. One veteran sales consultant at Ethan Allen, for example, noted that $1,000 could buy you a couch made from lower-quality fabric that wouldn't wear as well as a more expensive fabric. For maximum durability, all of our salespeople seemed to agree that you should aim to find a longer-wearing, quality fabric such as chenille, velvet, Ultrasuede, or leather, even though such fabrics tend to be expensive.

Interestingly, every one of the salespeople at the five retail giants I visited agreed that factors unrelated to quality can also increase the price of a couch. For example, where such features as fabric, size, style, and overall construction quality are equal between two pieces, the name of a well-known designer or manufacturer attached to the piece can make one piece substantially more expensive than another.

Not all of our salespeople were in agreement, however, as to whether construction and padding variations necessarily make a $5,000 couch a better-quality alternative to a $1,000 piece. A saleswoman at Marshall Field's, for example, informed me that $1,000 sofas generally will not have as much padding on the arms, and will usually have lighter-weight frames than $5,000 couches. A salesman I met at Thomasville, however, did not agree with her: he claimed that a $5,000 couch wouldn't necessarily have any more padding than a $1,000 couch. No wonder furniture shoppers are so confused! The saleswoman at Field's, however, did raise an interesting point regarding the construction of a couch's legs. She said that the legs of a more-expensive sofa usually aren't screwed into the piece; instead, they are carefully glued to the frame. In addition, all of the salespeople agreed that more-expensive couches are generally made with longer-lasting, eight-point hand-tied springs. The term "eight-point" refers to the fact that a spring is hand-tied eight times to ensure that the piece is strong and won't weaken with frequent usage.

At Furnitureland South in High Point, North Carolina—one of the largest and oldest retail furniture stores in the nation—I met a saleswoman named Carolyn who told me that, while there would be solid corner blocks used to reinforce the strength of the frame in more expensive sofas, some lower-priced couches also featured this same kind of reinforcement. Carolyn also mentioned a great tip on which I have always relied when testing cushions on upholstered goods, but which many salespeople don't know: with a less expensive couch, you should always observe whether the cushion rises up with you when you go from a sitting to a standing position. The better the spring mechanism on a piece, the more its cushions should move with your body. Most less expensive cushions, Carolyn noted, are filled with polyfoam.

Another great tip that Carolyn passed along to me, which I have shared with clients in the past, is this: if you can't afford a couch costing several thousand dollars, buy a couch in the $1,000 range. Then, when the cushioning gets flatter over time, take your cushions to an upholstery store and have the filling replaced—a far less expensive alternative to buying a $5,000 couch!

A Decent $1,000 Dresser: Is It Possible?

Many people also have asked me what they should look for when buying furniture made from wood. To help answer these questions, I decided to hear what our furniture retailing experts had to say about $1,000 dressers versus $5,000 dressers.

Andy, our reliable salesman back at Thomasville, told me that he could help me find a decent $1,000 dresser, and that a Thomasville dresser in this price range would be made using a combination of solids and veneers. Like several other salespeople I consulted at the same store, Andy recommended that I buy a dresser with dovetailing, or carved-out grooves, on the edges of its drawers. Dovetailing ensures that all the parts of a dresser will fit together perfectly, much like a puzzle. For added strength, Andy also recommended wood glides, which are stronger than metal glides. He noted, however, that a piece with both dovetailing and wood glides will generally be more expensive than a dresser in the $1,000 range.

At Ethan Allen, my salesperson told me that the store's more expensive dressers—that is, dressers well beyond the $1,000 price range—were more labor-intensive, and would generally either be over-sized or feature hand-painting, extensive carving, or veneering.

Ironically, a salesperson at Marshall Field's told me that the better and more expensive dressers offer deeper drawers than the less expensive dressers. *Huh? I don't think I quite agree with that theory!* I have seen plenty of dressers with deep drawers and flimsy construction, as well as dressers with shallower drawers that were very strong and well designed.

While all the retailers with whom I spoke concurred that it is possible to find a decent dresser for $1,000, Carolyn, our salesperson from Furnitureland South, said that better-quality dressers generally do cost more than $1,000. In fact, Carolyn went on to explain, the majority of Furnitureland South's good-quality dressers sell for more than $1,200. She also added, however, that Furnitureland South has recently begun carrying a line of dressers by Kincaid that are strong and built to last for around $1,200.

Carolyn gave me very detailed, careful answers about what to look for when buying a dresser—answers that I believe will be of great practical use to potential buyers. First, she recommended that buyers check for a dust cover between drawers—an added shelf used to support the drawers and prevent a drawer or its contents from falling through to the other drawers. Like Andy from Thomasville, Carolyn also noted the importance of opting for a dresser crafted with dovetailing. While dovetailing—grooves carved into the wood to secure the drawers—tends to be an expensive feature, it is a far more effective method than gluing for keeping the drawers strong. Carolyn also cautioned me against the veneers that are sometimes used in the construction of less expensive dressers. These veneers are flimsy, she noted, and won't last over time. She also brought up a useful tip that I mentioned earlier in this chapter: Be sure to pull a dresser's drawers in and out to make sure they glide smoothly. Finally, Carolyn noted that the front of a chest should be heavy and strong to withstand the weight of what is inside its drawers.

Reflections on My Experience: Testing the Retailers

While there definitely exists a relationship between the quality of furniture and its price, today's furniture buyer should nonetheless be able to find a satisfactory furniture choice in the lower price range. Indeed, my extensive research with retailers has shown that it is often perfectly reasonable to choose a $1,000 piece over a $5,000 piece, so long as you are well informed about the differences between them.

Another point worth considering is that, unlike a person buying furniture in the mid-1900s, today's consumer does not necessarily plan to keep the same furniture for fifty or more years. As Carolyn from Furnitureland South so cleverly noted, a consumer willing to forego the thicker padding in a pricey upholstered piece can engage in a cost-efficient cushion face-lift a few years down the road. Today's consumers, who are by no means stuck with their furniture choices for the rest of their lives, can thus save a bundle by purchasing less expensive pieces today, and upgrading or making improvements on those pieces tomorrow.

Another reason for consumers to opt for less expensive pieces is the fact that most shoppers today are not looking for suites of perfectly coordinated furniture. Instead, furniture shoppers may wish to put away extra furniture dollars to buy a new piece or two every few years, in order to keep up with changing tastes and styles. In addition, many of today's furniture buyers move frequently, and the cost of moving furniture—and the fact that the old stuff may not go with the look of the new place—is thus likely to affect buying decisions for many consumers.

If retailers want to survive in this highly competitive industry, they will have to better explain their pricing and construction details to consumers. While the majority of the salespeople at the five retail stores I visited were very helpful in answering my questions about price differentials between pieces, a few among them were not so cooperative. In addition, my ongoing undercover reviews of retail stores across the country confirm that many salespeople are not particularly helpful when it comes to answering shoppers' questions about price differences. My experience has taught me that many retailers won't be able to tell you what to look for in a piece, or what price you should pay, for a variety of reasons, ranging from ignorance to profit motive or lack of time. Some salespeople have become hostile over my questions simply because they haven't known the answers—they've looked at me as though I was deliberately putting them through the wringer. Others haven't taken the time because they simply can't spare it—or, more frustratingly, because they don't want to bother.

I don't necessarily fault *all* salespeople for their lack of knowledge or helpfulness when it comes to pricing, because many of them are simply following the leads of management. I do, however, fault the management and owners of these stores for not properly educating their sales staff about the basic construction and key features of the furniture they sell. I believe that, in addition to educating salespeople about their store's inventory, management should also be educating them about the competition's inventory. Such competitive information would help salesclerks make informed and sound comparisons between their own stock and that of their competitors—and would greatly increase their chances of making sales.

REDFLAG*

To Spend or Not to Spend?—What to Remember When Shopping at Retail Stores:

> The size and fabric of an upholstered piece will affect its final price.

> A piece made by a well-known designer can be more expensive than a piece made by an unknown designer.

> More expensive sofas should not have legs screwed into the frame; instead, the legs should be glued.

> Look for eight-point, hand-tied springs.

> When buying a less expensive sofa, know that you can always upgrade cushions over time.

> Check dressers to make sure they have dovetailing, wood glides, and dust covers between the drawers.

I hope that the future brings a better-trained sales force to the furniture industry, so that the brick wall often separating the American shopper from his ability to make smarter furniture choices will soon be a thing of the past.

5

The Styles and the Stylish

A History of Furniture Trends

Having spent years observing how all different kinds of people shop for furniture, whether in my own store or someone else's, I have observed one common thread that all furniture shoppers share: they will often hold back when it comes to labeling or even describing pieces of furniture, for fear they will incorrectly name the pieces or use the wrong lingo when identifying their parts. I've also noticed that whenever people are shopping for antiques, they become extremely unnerved and timid when it comes to talking about specifics of a piece—for example, its period or country of origin.

You should know that even the most well-renowned appraisers at the nation's top auction houses admit they have difficulty describing pieces that are not within their areas of expertise. I experienced this difficulty firsthand in one of my first assignments at Sotheby's, when I had to research several pictures of upholstered pieces that were supposedly designed by John Henry Belter, a famous furniture designer and craftsman who came to New York from Germany in the mid-1800s. The majority of Belter's pieces were ornately carved laminated rosewood suites, often upholstered in red velvet. Every day Sotheby's received several pictures from people who were convinced that their pieces were made by Belter. As part of our preliminary research, I was asked to come up with some accurate dating features and other qualitative ways of determining the identities of the pieces in the photos. Not only did I find this job extremely boring, but I also had recurring nightmares about people asking me to explain all the different ways you could tell whether furniture was designed by Belter! In real life, of course, no dealer or friend will ever test you like this—if you're lucky!

Although even Einstein wouldn't be expected to describe a piece with which he wasn't familiar, keep in mind that the more knowledgeable you appear to a dealer, the better the deal you may be able to strike. In fact, there are a few simple but critical things you can do to better prepare yourself for buying antiques, 20th-century furniture, or contemporary furniture.

Above all, before going furniture shopping, I recommend doing a little bit of research on the kind of furniture you are interested in purchasing. Get a feel for the prices, dating, and even the basic construction features of the types of pieces you will be encountering. Price guide books and recent auction sale prices are helpful, because they can give you an idea of the price you should expect to pay for the kind of furniture you want to buy—though you should know that these sources are not always accurate predictors of the price you will pay. All too often people ask me what I think of a piece *after* they've bought it. "I bought this piece. I was told it was made by so and so and from this or that country ... what do you think?" In these situations, I always think they would have been wiser to ask my opinion *beforehand*—or to have performed other research about the type of furniture they wished to buy, whether through books, online, or otherwise. If you are buying antiques, auction houses can also be wonderful resources—in fact, if you call an auction house on the telephone to ask what a similar piece went for at the most recent auction, they will generally tell you.

Remember: The more information you have about the furniture you are interested in buying, the better—because in the end it's you, the buyer, who must assume responsibility for your purchases. While reviewing stores incognito for my book, *Furniture Hot Spots*, I had a memorable experience that really drove home for me the significance of this "golden rule" of furniture shopping. I visited a store in Los Angeles that sells some very expensive and elegant Italian furniture from the early to mid-1950s. In a pile of furniture in the back of the store, a clear acrylic table caught my eye—largely because of its hefty $5,000 price tag. I knew it was time to take on the role of Agatha Christie's detective Hercule Poirot and do a little investigating as to why the price was so high! Other than looking a little rickety, the table had no visible signs of wear, nor did it look the least bit discolored from age. In fact, the hardware used on the table looked brand new. I asked the dealer to explain the piece, and to tell me why it was priced so high. He said that another dealer down the street had told him that the table was an American piece from the early 1900s, and thus worthy of that price. He then went on to admit he that knew nothing about the piece, or even why it was believed to be early American. But he sure did know how to mark up its price!

Because I know something about vintage Lucite—or acrylic—furniture, I knew that if the table had been made when the dealer claimed, it would have shown marked discoloration from age and imperfections from wear. I also knew that the kind of modern technology and hardware used in the construction of the table was not available at the time the dealer claimed it had been made—a dead giveaway that the table was a fake. As a result of being a buyer who did a little homework, I was able to walk confidently away from this piece and its hefty price tag. Perhaps more importantly, I also knew not to trust the dealer.

To prevent you from embarrassing yourself at cocktail parties and in your future interactions with furniture dealers, I have compiled some facts and tips that will help you become acquainted with the world of furniture. I can't tell you how many people have told me over the years that their house is decorated with French Provincial—when in reality the house looks more like English Country! Because it's so commonplace for people to confuse one period with another, I decided it was time to finally take the guesswork out of period pieces. What follows is a furniture timeline that will help you to keep it all straight—from dates to historical events and distinguishing characteristics of pieces from various periods. Study it before you shop, or take the book along with you on your next shopping trip so you can dazzle the dealers!

The Furniture of Royals

Since time immemorial, people have always been interested in what the royals have to say. In the realm of furniture, many of the "antiques" we know and love were commissioned by royals, which have made them endless sources of fascination for furniture shoppers throughout the ages. While most monarchs didn't create their own furniture designs, they did hire architects and cabinetmakers whose taste they admired. Guilds, or trade organizations, for furniture makers controlled how furniture was made, and these guilds in turn followed orders from their monarchs.

Humans have long been emotionally involved with their furnishings, and the world's great leaders have been no exception. Egypt's King Tutankhamen left an amazingly well-preserved collection of furniture, especially his Throne Chair, which dates to 1352 B.C. and was entombed with him after his death. Winston Churchill loved his easy chair. President Kennedy loved his famous rocking chair, and was so fond of the White House Resolute Desk that he moved it into the Oval Office in 1961. Throughout history, the world's greatest figures have been defined in various ways by the furniture they loved. Cabinetmaking is not something recent—as early as 3100 B.C. we were already well on our way to mastering the basic principles of fine woodworking.

The Furniture of Ancient Times: You Can't Take It with You . . . or Can You?

Although many wonderful furniture relics from the past have been ravaged by the passage of time, we have nonetheless been left with detailed drawings of household furniture from the earliest periods in human history. In fact, many early tombs depict drawings of furniture on slabs of stone. These drawings of the deceased's furniture tell us much about the past lives of the mysterious mummies that lie within, though they also leave many questions unanswered: Was the furniture worthy of a High Priestess? Did it bear the ebony, gold, and ivory accents worthy of a nobleman, or was it the simple furniture that most likely belonged to an ordinary citizen?

The 17th and 18th Centuries: Furniture to Die for

If we compare the excessive and luxurious furniture of 17th- and 18th-century French noblemen with the sparse, simple furnishings of the French masses from the same era, we can quickly grasp the great socioeconomic disparities that existed at this period in human history—the vast gulf between the aristocratic, privileged few and the majority of ordinary people. In fact, the enormous lifestyle disparity demonstrated by the contrast between the furniture of these two classes provides us with a great deal of insight and a greater understanding as to why many French aristocrats eventually lost their heads during the French Revolution that began in 1789. As is the case with all periods throughout history, the furniture of the time has a truly fascinating story to tell.

The 19th Century: In Search of a Comfortable Chair

In describing how people buy furniture, a good friend of mine once remarked, "At the end of the day, people just want to have a comfortable chair." This is true … unless you lived during the early 19th century. If you were a time traveler dropping in for a hot game of charades in the drawing room of a grand 19th-century English home, how do you think you might describe the furniture you saw? Luxurious? Opulent? Not! Truth be told, while the charades game might be hot, the furniture would be—by today's standards, anyway—downright uncomfortable. Indeed, much pre-19th-century furniture seemed expressly designed to be uptight and inhospitable—and those were its good points!

During the 19th century, stiff, dowdy furniture was considered an important reflection of the moral fabric of its owners; comfortable furniture was a sign of weak character! A similarly outdated belief held that bad posture would prevent a woman from finding a spouse. If you were craving the sort of comfort that today would be satisfied by a couch, your only comfortable option would be an ottoman. Needless to say, furniture was rarely designed or built with comfort in mind! Consider, for example, the following excerpt from Anthony Trollope's Victorian novel *Can You Forgive Her?*, which describes the mind-set of an early 19th-century English society lady toward furniture.

> She had been educated at a time when easy chairs were considered vicious and among people who regarded all easy postures as being so; and she could still boast, at seventy-six, that she had never leaned back. The vast majority of the prudent and oh so sensible British believed the softer and more comfy furniture such as easy chairs and other padded pieces were the cause of a wide range of ills from back maladies to, bite your tongue, bad posture; a condition certain to lessen the marketability of any young English lady for marriage faster than if she were caught unchaperoned in the company of a gentleman with (horrors!) his arm around her waist.

Comfort didn't really come into play until later in the 19th century, when springs were invented. Once springs and stuffing were used to make furniture, the couches became deeper and more comfortable.

Furniture Styles

THE ENGLISH (1700s TO 1900s)

William and Mary

When
Late 1600s, during the reign of William and Mary

Features
First appearance of upholstered furniture; walnut replaces oak; floral designs carved in wood; Windsor chair

A Royal Dutchman Takes a Child Bride
Considering that furniture styles during the reign of William and Mary (1688–1702) served as the inspiration for pieces being made both in England and throughout the colonial New World until at least 1725, it seems only fitting that we should get to know these royals better by examining their private lives.

William and Mary had an odd marriage. In fact, if its members were alive today, their royal family could easily have competed on the TV show *Family Feud*. One of the hardest parts of William and Mary's marriage was their twelve-year age difference. William had many lady friends during their tumultuous marriage, though Mary worked hard to preserve their relationship, and even began a campaign to win over her Dutch husband by learning his ways so she could better please him.

After a royal squabble in which William and Mary overthrew Mary's father, the newly crowned King James II, the couple assumed for themselves the roles of joint rulers of England. Over the years, Mary and William seemed to grow quite fond of one another, and proved to be exemplary co-rulers worthy of England's crown. When William was away at battle, Mary tended to the nation like a confident, autonomous queen. When he returned, she dutifully returned to him the responsibility of running the country, resuming her role as the dutiful wife. Despite their mutual understanding, however, William never ceased his constant visits to the quarters of one of Mary's ladies-in-waiting.

With respect to furniture design, the reign of William and Mary was marked by a more comfortable and fashionable flair than had characterized the previous Jacobean period. Exotic walnut woods came into vogue, replacing the oak that had previously been common. Lines and form became less severe, and floral inlaid carvings, detailed scrolls, and lacquer finishes became the unique touches of the period. Perhaps most significant during this period, however, was William and Mary's introduction of upholstered pieces. In addition, wing chairs were constructed for the first time. Not only were these chairs attractive, with their wings covered in fashionable fabrics, but they were also functional, since they protected the persons who sat in them from getting chilled by the drafty houses of the period.

Queen Anne

When
Early 1700s, during the reign of Queen Anne

Features
Invention of highboys and the famous Queen Anne chair; cupboards; shell motifs

Georgian

When
Most of the 18th century after 1715, during the reigns of the three King Georges

Features
Mahogany wood; claw-and-ball feet used at the ends of legs; introduction of rich upholstery; invention of the sideboard; cabriole legs on chairs and tables

Famous Designers
Thomas Chippendale, Robert Adam, Hepplewhite and Sheraton

Chippendale

When
1740 to 1779

Features
English interpretation of Chinese furniture designs; latticework on chairs and tables; extensive carving and cutout backs; French Rococo–inspired designs

Famous Designer
Thomas Chippendale

English Regency

When
Late 1700s to early 1800s, during the regency of George IV

Features
Continuation of styles from the early 1700s; furniture resembles that of the French Directoire period (late 1700s) and Empire period (early 1800s); simpler, smaller scale furniture than in previous periods; inspired by Chinese and Egyptian motifs; some chairs have caning as seats; lacquered frames and exotic designs

Famous Designer
Thomas Sheraton

Bad Boy King George IV
The eldest son of King George III, the reigning monarch at the time of the American Revolution was born George Frederick Augustus. But this future heir to the throne—and life of the party—preferred to be called by his nickname, Prinnie. Prinnie's outrageous behavior and pranks made him a favorite target for caricatures and embarrassing stories.

Despite the fact that he was born into a life of royal privilege and wealth, one cannot help but feel rather sorry for Prinnie. His father, George III, suffered from unpredictable bouts of madness. And after each episode, just when Prinnie was finally prepared to ascend the throne, his father would miraculously recover! Prinnie dated many royals, but eventually fell in love with and married Maria Fitzherbert in 1786. The union was declared illegal by his father because Prinnie had never asked for permission to marry, and also because the bride was Catholic—which by that time was not allowed in England, thanks to Henry VIII. Instead, Prinnie was encouraged by his father to marry Caroline of Brunswick, his cousin. It is reported that Prinnie, after taking one look at Caroline, immediately retired to his apartment and called out for a brandy, complaining for hours that he felt ill.

Despite his personal trials, however, Prinnie was fortunate to have lived during the Regency Period—a liberal age in which art, fashion, furniture, and romance flourished. When he was sober, this Prince Regent was extremely charming and refined, with a great appreciation and taste for all the finest trappings of culture—especially furniture. In fact, he spared no expense when it came to furnishing his residences. He commissioned the most gifted artists of the Regency Period—including the architect John Nash and the furniture designer Henry Holland—to overhaul his bachelor pad, Carlton House, which was a mansion just off Pall Mall in London, and his royal seaside home, Brighton Pavilion. Both homes were filled with the most exquisite furniture—an eclectic mix of classical Roman, Egyptian, Indian, and Eastern influences—and included famous Regency pieces like rosewood sideboards mounted on gilded dragons that bore great silver candelabras.

Victorian

When
1837 to 1901, during the reign of Queen Victoria

Features
Introduction of machine-made furniture; red velvet upholstery; springs in sofas and chairs; heavy frames ; popularity of mahogany and walnut; resemblance to French Rococo; horsehair used to make cushions

Famous Designers

Edward William Godwin, William Morris, Augustus Pugin, Philip Webb

Arts and Crafts

When

Early 1900s, beginning in England

Features

Also known as "Mission Style," a reference to styles seen in California missions; straight lines; oak wood; airy, rustic looks with exposed hardware; functional designs; minimal orna-mentation; brass tacks; leather

Famous Designers

William Morris, Gustav Stickley, Roycroft Industries

THE FRENCH (1600s TO 1900s)

Louis XIII

When

First half of the 17th century, during the reign of Louis XIII

Features

Pieces designed by furniture guilds at the instruction of monarchs; twisted legs; cabinets divided into two parts; fancy carvings

Louis XIV

When

1643 to 1715

Features

Also known as the Baroque period; pieces designed by furniture guilds with the input of the monarchs; straight legs; high-backed chairs; carved oak and walnut; upholstery; marble-topped console tables; gilding

The Sun King: Louis XIV

Few royals in history had egos that could rival that of Louis XIV, who broke all records with his seventy-two-year reign! In fact, this self-absorbed sovereign gave new meaning to the term "egotist." He was dubbed the "Sun King" because, in the political scheme of the French state, he was the center of all power—everything revolved around him, just as the planets in our solar system revolve around and draw their energy from the sun.

The architecture of Louis XIV's famous chateau, Versailles, is reflective of his enormous power. The public side of the chateau consists of a series of balconies that draw the viewer's eye to the center of the palace. At the exact center of the structure is the king's balcony, where Louis XIV would speak to crowds assembled in the courtyards below. Louis not only had the distinction of having the entire 17th century dubbed the "Age of Louis" in his honor, but he also had the vision to turn run-down Versailles—a hunting retreat built by Louis XIII—into a magnificent palace. Versailles became the largest royal palace in Europe, a symbol of the widespread social, cultural, and political influence of France in the 17th and 18th centuries.

When it came to furnishings, Louis spared no expense in transforming Versailles into a magnificent palace. He wanted the house to be a showplace for the entire world—in part to showcase the social and cultural power of France—so he appointed the famous artist Monsieur Le Brun as the official director of the Manufacture Royale des Meubles de la Couronne, where all the furniture for Versailles was to be made. The furniture designs Louis chose were elaborate and highly detailed. Among the notable pieces he selected were transitional wardrobes and tall dressers made from carved oak and featuring amazing inlays of masks, a collection of over 400 exquisite beds "fit for a Sun King," and hundreds of gilded chairs, screens, and tables. Louis XIV was so proud of Versailles that he opened his palace to visiting dignitaries from all over the world so they could observe firsthand every detail of his splendid life.

Louis XV

When
1715 to 1774, during the reign of Louis XV

Features
Also known as "Rococo"; fancy, ornate furniture with a feminine style; extensive curves and scrollwork; bombé chests; cabriole legs; emphasis on comfort and extensive use of colors; extensive gilding; quality and construction controlled by guilds

Famous Designers
Madame de Pompadour (Louis XV's mistress), Mathieu Criard, Charles Cressent

Madame de Pompadour: Louis XV's Mistress
Madame de Pompadour was a beautiful woman who married young, then left her husband after a brief marriage when she met Louis XV at a ball. She ended up moving into Versailles to live in special quarters designed for her by the king—complete with a secret passageway leading to his quarters. Pompadour was a free spirit, and wasn't afraid to tell Louis what he should do with respect to his job. She loved anything having to do with decorative arts—from furniture to china—and she shared her love of the arts with Louis, who allowed her to have free reign over the decoration of Versailles.

In her work at Versailles, Madame de Pompadour introduced feminine, smaller-scale furniture with luscious pastels such as green and pink. She loved flowers, and blended floral motifs into the Rococo furniture designed for the palace. Her style became known as the "Pompadour style." Recently her apartments and furnishings at Versailles underwent an overhaul, restoring them to their former glory.

Louis XV: Ladies' Man

Louis XV outshone both Louis XIV and Louis XVI in affairs of state . . . and I'm not referring to official business! Despite the fact that his queen, the former Marie Leczinska of Poland, was an unappealing woman, Louis managed to produce ten children with her. And although he was busy with all of these children, he also kept busy with numerous lady friends. His most well-known lover was Madame de Pompadour, whose influence over the furniture design at Versailles was more significant than that of the king himself.

Louis XVI

When

1774 to 1792, during the reign of Louis XVI and his wife, Marie Antoinette

Features

Rectilinear style; square legs; pieces not overly decorated; column-style legs; gilding; fabrics with gold and white stripes

Famous Designers

Georges Jacob, Jean-Henri Riesener

Marie Antoinette: Louis XVI's Wife

Marie Antoinette, an Austrian archduchess, came from a family of sixteen children. Her mother, Maria Theresa, told Marie Antoinette at a young age that she had arranged a marriage between Marie Antoinette and Louis XVI in an effort to ally Austria and France. When she was only fourteen, Marie Antoinette moved to France to marry Louis XVI.

Even though this historic pair is best known for losing their heads in the French Revolution, there are many other juicy behind-the-scenes facts to explore about their fascinating lives.

"Madame Deficit," as Marie Antoinette became known to her countrymen, was a spoiled girl, notorious for spending incredible sums of money on clothing, jewels, gambling, and anything else that struck her fancy, even at a time when the great masses of France lived hand-to-mouth on the brink of starvation. Despite the fact that Marie performed some acts of charity for the poor, even occasionally contributing money, for the most part she used her country's riches to further her and Louis XVI's decadent lifestyle at court.

The extravagance of the royal pair's lifestyle is evident from the furniture that they chose. Marie favored a romantic and delicate look in her furniture, and she spared no expense in commissioning some of the most talented artists of the period to realize her vision. Tapered legs became simpler in line than the traditional cabriole legs of the past. Changes can also be seen in the color and ornamentation of the pieces Marie commissioned, as heavy ornate carvings and gilt were replaced with furniture painted in soft white and accented with dainty decorations. Jean-Henri Riesener, one of the most famed artists of the period, created for Marie an exceptional desk embellished with flowers and the trophies of battle. Another skilled artist, the cabinetmaker G. Benneman, created for Marie two amazing buffets of superb detail that now reside in the Louvre.

Although today the French admire and treasure the furniture of Louis XVI and Marie Antoinette, this was not the case during their reign. On the contrary, these pieces did little more than breed contempt on the part of the masses for the opulent lifestyles of their rulers—a sentiment that eventually contributed significantly to the royal couple's fateful meeting with the guillotine.

French Provincial

When
Late 1600s to 1800s

Features
Furniture made in French provinces; rustic look; relatively inexpensive; made from local woods such as walnut and pine; some designs imitate those produced in cities for aristocrats; popular styles include Windsor and ladder-back chairs

French Empire

When
1804 to 1815, during the reign of Napoleon and his wife, Josephine

Features
Asian-influenced designs incorporating Egyptian and Greek motifs; fancy but simple lines; marble tabletops; metal feet; mahogany and rosewood; motifs signifying the empire: lions, sphinxes, eagles, "N"

Famous Designers
Charles Percier, Pierre Fontaine

Napoleon and Josephine: "Power Is My Mistress"

Napoleon and Josephine have become legendary as two invincible soul mates that seemed destined for one another, and who seemed to have it all—including a vast empire. If we explore beyond the pages of the typical history book, however, and dare to enter the closed doors of Napoleon and Josephine's private chambers, we learn that the relationship between this poor boy from Corsica and the sophisticated, aristocratic woman of his dreams was far from ideal. When their famous relationship began, Josephine had not exactly been sitting idly around awaiting her Prince Charming. On the contrary, Josephine was a thirty-three-year-old widow—her aristocratic husband had inconveniently lost his head in the French Revolution—with a penchant for love affairs with powerful politicians, including one of the most important men in French government, Paul Barras.

Although Napoleon was not considered handsome and was rather pudgy—and, of course, too short—the blue-blooded Josephine nonetheless decided to seize upon the feisty, up-and-coming young general. Perhaps her eagerness to marry had something to do with the fact that, back in those days, fifteen was considered the ideal age for females to wed—and, to put it bluntly, Josephine wasn't getting any younger. Early letters written by Napoleon while he was away at war reveal a man driven by a fiery passion for his adorable bride. His later letters, however, express a hostility stemming from resentment and suspicion about why she did not regularly write back to him.

Eventually Napoleon's doubts about Josephine's fidelity proved true when he discovered that she was carrying on with a dashing young lieutenant. As revenge, Napoleon took a string of mistresses, bitterly commenting that "my mistresses do not in the least engage my feelings. Power is my mistress." Napoleon divorced the childless Josephine when she was forty so he could, as he put it, "marry a womb" and produce a child. Despite their volatile marriage and subsequent separation, however, upon her death Napoleon lamented that she was "the only woman I have truly loved."

Despite the fact that Napoleon came from humble beginnings in a Corsican village, he developed a great taste for and knowledge of the fine arts. In fact, his enjoyment of refined living spawned an entire line of furniture known as "campaign furniture"—portable pieces including folding chairs, small chests, and even bathtubs, that could be taken apart and transported to reproduce the comforts of civilized living for Napoleon as he roughed it abroad on the battlefield.

Napoleon wanted his home, Malmaison, to have the finest furnishings, and during their marriage he gave Josephine a free hand when it came to decorating. Convinced that his furniture needed to reflect the grandeur of his status as the ruler of a vast empire, he preferred pieces with a larger-than-life style—massive, heavy, regal pieces fashioned after pieces from the Greek, Egyptian, and Roman empires, and adorned with lions, sphinxes, and female figures. Pieces in Napoleon's preferred style, dubbed "Empire Furniture," influenced the furniture styles of the entire country.

Art Nouveau

When
1890 to 1910

Features
Asymmetrical designs; free-form carved woods; nature symbols, including flowers, plants, and animals; ironwork that twists and turns

Famous Designers
Hector Guimard, Victor Horta, Henry van de Velde, Gustave Serrurier-Bovy

Art Deco

When
1908 to 1930

Features
Shorter legs on seated furniture; luxurious fabrics made from silk; exotic woods such as ebony, amboyna, and pallisander; steel, leather, and glass introduced; enamel; mother-of-pearl; sophisticated styles

Famous Designers
Le Corbusier, Pierre Chareau, Louis Majorelle, Jacques Émile Ruhlmann

Art Moderne

When
1925 to 1940

Features
Similar in style to Art Deco, but with more extreme and angular designs; incorporates designs of international designers and transitions Art Deco style into the mid-20th century

THE AMERICANS (1600s TO 1900s)

Colonial

When

1600s to 1700s

Features

Began with simple and practical pieces; chests and trestle tables in English styles; cedar and pine furniture made mostly in New Jersey, New York, and Pennsylvania; later styles are more ornate and resemble Queen Anne, Chippendale, and French designs; Windsor chairs

Shaker

When

Late 1700s to early 1800s

Features

Handmade furniture made by an American religious group living in small villages along the East Coast; no decoration; extreme functionality; swivel chairs and stools; pine; pieces resemble French Provincial

American Federal

When
Late 1700 to mid-1800s

Features
Includes American Empire furniture; inspired by French Empire but heavier in size; legs straight; fronts of cabinets and chairs curved; mahogany wood

Famous Designer
Duncan Phyfe

Mission

When
1895 to 1910

Features
Furniture made in Southern California using dark-stained oak originally; inspired by Arts and Crafts movement; simple designs with block legs; straight legs with stretchers; functionality of paramount importance

Famous Designers
Roycroft Industries, Gustav Stickley, Frank Lloyd Wright

OTHER KEY PERIODS

Biedermeier

When
1815 to 1830

Features
Furniture designed in Austria and Germany; folk style rejecting previous European styles; simple lines; functional designs; legs tapered or straight; emphasis on wood grains; maple, birch, ash, and fruitwoods; contemporary styling; reproduced by the Swedes in the late 1800s

Famous Designers
Josef Danhauser, Karl Friedrich Schinkel

Modern Movement (Includes Bauhaus and Retro)

When
Early to mid-1900s

Features

Functional furniture made around the world; accessories important; popular designs to fit everyday lives; plastic, metal,
and bentwood are common materials

Famous Designers

Bertoia, Marcel Breuer, Le Corbusier, Eames, Gio Ponti, Eero
Saarinen, Mies van der Rohe

6

From the Mouths of Experts

Top Designers
Share
Their Insights
and Secrets

n today's era of reality television, we have all seen a TV host demonstrate how easy it is to transform an ordinary house into a magnificent showplace in one week's time. And of course the whole thing is pulled off with amazing ease and on an incredibly modest budget, with the majority of the furnishings supplied by well-known national chain stores. And who among us hasn't thumbed through dozens of magazines, circling pictures of our favorite "rooms," with visions of re-creating the same looks—right down to the very pictures on the wall? Unfortunately, putting together a house that will please our palate, match our lifestyle, and fit our budget is a bit more complicated in real life.

Most of us can't hire an entire TV "dream team" of consultants to advise us, and many of us don't wish to employ a designer—either because of the cost, or because we prefer to try our own hand at decorating. However, because so many people seem interested in watching the nation's best interior designers and absorbing what they say, I thought I would share with you some of their stories and tips. To accomplish this, I conducted personal interviews with twelve highly regarded interior designers—Kim Alexandriuk, Robin Bell, Alessandra Branca, John Gregory, Kerry Joyce, Miles Redd, Harriet Robinson, Todd Alexander Romano, Travis Smith, Steven Volpe, and Willis Watts—each of whom has a different view of the design industry, and each of whom has his or her own unique ideas. So settle in, and join me for this rare chance to be a fly on the wall as I gather the secrets of the experts!

Backgrounds

You may be surprised to learn that many of these famous designers didn't have traditional training or schooling in interior design. Los Angeles celebrity designer Kerry Joyce, for example, initially designed sets for theaters and for acts like Tony Orlando and Dawn (remember them from "Tie a Yellow Ribbon Round the Old Oak Tree"?). Joyce has now moved on to designing homes for celebrities such as hotelier Ian Schrager and Tom Freston, the co-president of Viacom. Other designers developed a knack for the design business early in life. As a young kid growing up in southern Indiana, for example, John Gregory (who now lives in Dallas) taught himself everything he could about antiques by frequenting the many flea markets near his home. New York's Todd Alexander Romano actually began his career in men's fashion in New York City. These diverse backgrounds prove that creative spirits are never static; they are constantly evolving, and true artists are always expanding their creativity.

Advice to Those Just Starting Out

First-time furniture buyers intimidated by the cost of decorating their entire home at once often feel uncomfortable telling designers that they want to furnish their homes slowly. If you're a consumer who falls into this category, you don't need to worry. Designing a house slowly over time is not only financially wise, but also protects you from creating a quickly dated look. Filling an entire house with furniture all at once often creates an overly homogenous look, instead of a more personalized, eclectic look that is best achieved over time to reflect our changing lives and style.

Miles Redd, one of the top interior designers in New York City, suggests that those on a limited budget concentrate primarily on the "bones" of a house: the wall colors, flooring, and basic structural design features. "From great bones," he advises, "you can then add great furniture." Others, like Harriet Robinson, recommend getting an idea for the "final look" you want so you can proceed in a specific direction as you decorate.

As for reference materials, most good designers highly recommend referring to the popular *Franklin Report*—available in book form or online at *www.franklinreport.com*—which evaluates and rates the best contractors and interior designers in New York, Los Angeles, and Chicago. John Gregory warns that if you are hiring a designer, make sure you agree on color and find out if the use of color is one of that designer's strengths—otherwise you may make some real decorating mistakes. The *Franklin Report* may be able to help you answer this question as you research potential designers. In addition, Steven Volpe recommends reading newspapers like the *New York Times* and *Wall Street Journal* regularly—and, of course, the well-known decorating magazines—for unusual furniture ideas.

I have learned firsthand the problems that can arise if you select the wrong designer. Most importantly, make sure that you feel comfortable with the designer you choose. I strongly advise against choosing a decorator simply because he or she decorates the homes of all your friends, or because he or she has very wealthy clients. Some of the industry's most high-profile designers with the greatest status in the industry can also be the most challenging designers with whom to work.

Value: Getting the Most "Bang" for Your Buck

I began my interviews by asking our top designers to share the ways in which average consumers could get the most "bang" for their buck when furnishing their homes. Washington, D.C. designer Travis Smith, who has been heralded for his work in some of D.C.'s finest restaurants, clubs, businesses, and upscale homes, shared these insights:

> I am known for acquiring a lot of my furnishings from flea markets and antique stores. One of my favorite bargains was finding a pair of giant fiberglass Tiki totems for a club I designed in Virginia called Continental. I found them at a junk store in Philly for $200, and they ended up flanking the Tiki bar at the club. They became the center of attention, creating an absolute smash when the place opened. Other showstoppers I've created are the result of just letting my innate eclectic impulses run wild. Sometimes I will draw from my upbringing in the Southwest and meld this with the rustic, earthy elements of 1950s and '60s modern designs.

For new, eclectic furniture and accessories, Travis says that Urban Outfitters can't be beat!

Miles Redd, famous both for his exhilarating use of color and his creative edge, shared with me a wonderful tip for creating inexpensive table decorations. He suggested buying a pair of coral seashells for about $35, which he promised would add a "sculptural quality to any table setting." He also confided, "If you're on a small budget, then think color. Color can make all the difference. It can turn any house or room from basic ordinary to vibrant . . . Don't be afraid to take a risk, because if you do make a mistake, color can be easily corrected." Redd has received rave reviews for chasing away doldrums by dressing up kitchens with a coat of his favorite color: Tiffany Blue. He also claims that, when it comes to flooring, he loves two-toned patterns using classic Greek influences.

New York City's Robin Bell, a senior designer at McMillen—one of the oldest design companies in the country—also offers some extremely creative tips. Bell recommends that, instead of pitching those Val-Pak coupons that we all receive in the mail, we should take a closer look at them. She recounted to me how she once found a coupon from a closet company advertising custom-designed closets. A shrewd negotiator, Bell called the company and persuaded it to apply her coupon toward purchasing custom bookshelves by arguing that bookshelves were much simpler to make than a closet. Although the company hemmed and hawed, it ultimately consented! The lesson? Bargains can be found anywhere—even among your junk mail, where you least expect them!

Robin also shared a clever trick for creating an instant coat closet. Recently, when decorating a home that lacked a coat closet, Bell took several brass doorstops with rubber tips and placed them in a long row along the wall. She then removed the rubber tips to reveal the nice brass. Problem solved—and the look was a big success!

Finally, Bell provided an effective and value-conscious tip for covering up unsightly wood floors. For wood floors that are not in good shape and are too expensive to refinish, Bell suggests using bamboo matting, which can be cut to any size, to cover the floors. With double-sided carpet tape, she advises, you can make your floors look wonderful in no time.

Great Upholstered Goods for Less

While many of the designers I interviewed recommended auctions and flea markets for finding some good-quality used upholstered pieces, Robin Bell suggested visiting a retailer called Classic Sofa in New York (located at 5 West 22nd Street; contact the store by phone at 212-620-0485). According to Bell, "Classic Sofa does the most amazing job of making good-quality sofas in any price range. Another benefit besides their unbeatable prices is that Classic Sofa will make any sofa in two weeks and ship anywhere in the U.S."

Far from his L.A. base, Kerry Joyce loves to visit CS Post (*www.cspost.com*), a "Pottery Barn–like store based in Hays, Kansas." Nationally, he finds Mitchell Gold sofas a good value, and notes that you can find Mitchell Gold products at Crate & Barrel and Pottery Barn locations throughout the U.S. For good-quality, reasonably priced sofas in Los Angeles, Joyce says that Shelter can't be beat.

When it comes to flea market finds, most people are not as lucky as designer Willis Watts, the owner of Delaware River Trading Company—a popular Atlanta home furnishings store that has been featured in many top magazines. One day while cherry-picking through flea market items, Willis stumbled upon twenty-four bankers' chairs for a total of $6. While not every flea market visit will produce a bargain as dramatic as this, the lesson is that you never know what you'll find—so it never hurts to look!

Some designers, like Chicago designer Alessandra Branca, who is known for her wonderfully colorful and classically inspired interiors, believe—just as I believe—that you can indeed find great deals shopping retail. According to Branca, "I recently found the most wonderful slipper chair at Restoration Hardware. I was elated because it cost under $700. Just as special as the chair and its price, though, was the news that I could actually send my own fabric to Restoration Hardware to have the chair upholstered. The result: fabulous!"

Todd Alexander Romano, in keeping with true to his passion for antiques, says that he loves shopping in Paris and finding a "Napoleon III [mid- to late-19th-century] tufted chair, or something along those lines, for clients." Though we can't all go to Paris, we can nonetheless draw a little inspiration from the types of items that designers like Romano uncover in their travels.

Finding Impressive But Inexpensive Desk Lamps

On several occasions over the years, people have asked me where they can find a good-looking, functional desk lamp that isn't expensive. While I have suggested many good places to shop for desk lamps, both online and in chain stores such as IKEA and Ligne Roset, I wanted to compare notes with the experts, so I asked them to share their secrets.

When it comes to shedding a little light on the subject of desk lamps, Kim Alexandriuk—a prominent Los Angeles designer whose work has been shown in many magazines, including *House Beautiful*—recommends a line at Chelsea Passage of Barney's New York called R&Y Augousti. "They make incredible lamps, furniture, picture frames, etc., out of exotic materials like python and stingray. I purchased a desk lamp for a client, and it is stunning and was not expensive."

Harriet Robinson, a busy Chicago designer who works on many architecturally famous landmark homes, recommends Lightology at *www.lightology.com*, where you can choose from hundreds of desk lamps in a wide range of prices.

Alessandra Branca once again gives Restoration Hardware the thumbs-up, noting its varied selection and reasonable prices. She also recommends getting an articulated lamp for better positioning.

Miles Redd suggests Circa Lighting, which offers a great selection of lamps both in its Atlanta store and on its Web site (*www.circalighting.com*).

Kerry Joyce frequents Visual Comfort in Houston (by phone at 713-686-5999, or online at *www.visualcomfort.com*) for its great selection of lighting—and, in particular, its excellent selection of floor lamps, sconces, and desk lamps.

As an antiques buff, John Gregory prefers to scour vintage stores to find vintage lamps with "good lines" that he can have nickel-plated.

Todd Alexander Romano loves the good values he finds at Lee's Studios in New York (*www.leesstudios.com*).

Finally, Steven Volpe of Hedge in San Francisco recommends the lamps found in the new Williams-Sonoma Home catalog. He particularly likes the Thompson Drafting Lamp, which is crafted of solid brass with a polished nickel finish, "because of its versatility."

The Experts' Favorite Retail Stores

Many of us have shopped at big chain stores for at least some of the pieces in our homes. Most of the designers I interviewed also frequent stores such as Crate & Barrel, Pottery Barn, Restoration Hardware, IKEA, Williams-Sonoma Home, and Design Within Reach. In addition, the experts visit stores in various cities across the country, including: Terence Conran's in New York; ABC Carpet and Home in New York; Bergdorf Goodman in New York; Elliot's Hardware Store on Maple Avenue in Dallas; West Elm in New York, San Francisco, and Chicago; and CB2 in Chicago.

How Shoppers Can Avoid Getting Ripped off

According to Lee Stanton, a well-known antiques dealer in Los Angeles who swears he never buys antiques for his clients that he has not personally handpicked or that he would not consider owning himself, confided to me that his clients never feel ripped off—no matter how much they spend—provided that they've bought a "unique item that they love and will enjoy." The moral: taste is relative. If you like an item, the chances are great that you will enjoy it, and maybe even forget about exceeding your budget—at least for that one piece.

Nonetheless, whenever you buy a piece—especially from an antiques dealer—Willis Watts from Atlanta suggests doing some fact-checking to make sure you are not buying a knockoff. To learn more about furniture styles and designers, Willis recommends checking out the resources of the Cooper Hewitt Design Museum, located in the old Carnegie Mansion on New York's Upper East Side (2 East 91st Street; 212-849-8400; *www.si.edu/ndm*).

Here's a good tip about cyberspace auctions from Washington, D.C. designer Travis Smith:

> You can't be too careful on eBay when it comes to selecting sellers. Make sure to choose only those who have high levels of feedback with a positive rating. Look for those sellers who have a rating of at least 100 or more. You can read their entire history of customer feedback to find out how reliable they are.

I like that tip!

Finally, Todd Alexander Romano warns against getting "carried away" and overbidding at auctions. Romano firmly believes that if you are going to an auction, you should always set your upper price limit before the auction begins. Do your research, set limits, and stick to your guns—that way you won't regret your purchase once you get it home.

Couch Proportions: Some Rules of Thumb

While most designers don't have exact rules of thumb for selecting the couch size that will be perfectly proportioned to your room, New York's Robin Bell advises as follows:

> Don't be timid about picking the largest piece that the space will allow as an anchor for the room. Also, I recommend using the fewest number of cushions on a couch; otherwise the cushions look like Chiclets ... I want to give people a seam alert for couches. Most people really don't like sitting on seams, so the fewer seams on a couch the better.

Travis Smith cautions that "you really should factor chair size into the equation as well. Chairs should be equal in scale to your sofa so they are not dwarfed by the sofa."

Alessandra Branca is more specific in her requirements. A couch, she says, "should be no deeper than 20 inches in the seat or 22 inches in the frame. And for the back of the sofa, no higher than 34 inches."

Favorite Web Sites

I have found that designers generally do not shop online, nor do they recommend that their clients do so. One reason for this might be that furniture purchased online is more difficult to mark up! However, many designers justify the need to shop in person based on a desire to actually see and touch the pieces being purchased. Despite interior designers' resistance to shopping online, our top gun designers nonetheless offered some wonderful Web site alternatives to shopping in stores.

Travis Smith gives his stamp of approval to *www.modernica.net* for new reissue Mid-Century Modern pieces. He also recommends his own Web site at *www.goodeyeonline.com*—which I, myself, frequent—for vintage modern pieces. He adds, "Whenever I think 'online shopping,' eBay always comes to mind. It's a wonderful source where you can stumble on to some terrific deals. It's an all-around great place to look for just about anything."

Favorite chain store Web sites for our designer group include: Design Within Reach, West Elm, and Restoration Hardware.

For kids' furniture, Kim Alexandriuk recommends the Oakland, California–based contemporary online children's retail store, *www.modernseed.com.*

Kerry Joyce is one of the few designers in the country who has embraced furniture Web sites for ideas and purchases. Some of his absolute favorites include Pottery Barn's hip new West Elm, at *www.westelm.com*. He also loves Crate & Barrel's new Mod store, CB2's Web site at *www.cb2.com*, and *www.cspost.com* for wonderful sofas and chairs. Other favorites of Joyce include *www.conran.co.uk*, *www.noguchi.org*, *www.modernliving.com*, *www.modernica.com,* and *www.room.com.*

Favorite Flea Markets and Antiques Shows

As I interviewed these experienced and talented designers, it became apparent that all of them like to frequent flea markets and antiques shows in hope of finding a diamond in the rough. In fact, many of these designers confessed that their most memorable treasures come from such sources.

Favorite flea markets of both Alessandra Branca and Harriet Robinson include the Sandwich Fairgrounds, located in the small and quaint rural town of Sandwich, Illinois. Atlanta's Willis Watts says his markets of choice are the Brimfield, Massachusetts Flea Market (508-347-2761) and the Long Beach, California Flea Market—held on the third Sunday of every month, and not to be confused with the Rose Bowl Flea Market in Pasadena. Some of Travis Smith's top contenders include the Georgetown Flea Market in Washington, D.C. and the Double Toll Gate Flea Market located just outside of D.C. in Front Royal, Virginia. Smith is also partial to the Meadow Lands Flea Market, located not far outside Pittsburgh, Pennsylvania. In New York, Miles Redd swears by the Chelsea Annex (26th Street and 6th Avenue), held every Sunday.

Kerry Joyce, known for his one-of-a-kind picks in furniture venues, selected the Elephant's Trunk Country

Flea Market in Danbury, Connecticut (203-355-1448). Like designer Steven Volpe, he also loves the San Francisco Antique Show held in San Francisco every October.

For antiques shows, Travis Smith is a fan of the Scott Show in Columbus, Ohio, which specializes in country and shabby chic furnishings. The majority of our designers cited Pier 88 in the Triple Pier Expo in Manhattan, and the Winter Show at the Triple Pier. Kim Alexandriuk and Lee Stanton also mentioned the spectacular Marche Serpette flea market in Paris and the Olympia Fair in London. Steven Volpe loves the Paul Bert market in Paris.

As you can see, our designers do hit the flea markets in order find to unusual pieces and good deals, and you can do the same.

How Designers Charge

All of the designers I interviewed charge an hourly consultation fee, plus a commission on every item purchased. Generally, the more experienced the designer, the higher his or her hourly rate. The industry is changing, however, and designers recognize a need to reexamine how they charge their clients. A more fee-based arrangement will likely become an industry standard.

Thanks to the Web, today's end users (buyers) have more pricing knowledge than ever before. They also enjoy more options than ever for buying furniture, from the growing number of furniture Web sites and catalogs to the many new chain stores throughout the U.S.—such as IKEA and West Elm, which offer reasonably priced knockoffs and are easy to shop. In addition, many retail stores are becoming savvier marketers by offering features such as their own free, in-house design consultants or computer kiosks placed around their stores that allow customers to create entire rooms full of furnishings with just a click.

Some Over-the-Top Finishing Touches

Let's face it. We all want to live vicariously through the owners of those one-of-a-kind showcase homes that are splashed across the front covers of glossy design magazines. So here are some over-the-top, unforgettable touches created especially by our own designers:

Kim Alexandriuk: "I designed a 24-karat, gilt, hand-carved, Italian-style bed with a pink-and-chartreuse hand-sewn bed skirt and bedcover with glass beads, for a four-year-old girl's room." *I wonder what kind of bed she'll get for her sweet sixteen!*

John Gregory: "A chagrin leather lingerie cabinet on a silver-leaf stand, and silk-lined drawers with hand-knotted silk tassels."

Kerry Joyce: "One of my favorite projects was designing a bowling alley for a family. Accessed by an elevator, I created a wonderful bowling alley club that felt very much like a fantasy speakeasy. Smoked mirrors, mahogany paneling, the handsome beamed ceiling patina in a beautiful burnt orange, bar area, and arcade area—4,000 square feet of pure fantasy. I also did a pop-up TV at the foot of a bed in the master bedroom. To keep height to a minimum, I actually recessed part of the mechanism into the floor to mitigate the final height. I designed it to look like an incredible antique trunk, containing two plasma screens, back-to-back, one for the bed and one for the sitting area directly opposite of it." *Wow!!!*

Harriet Robinson: "I once ordered a desk and chair from Garouste and Bonetti in Paris, made with gilded bronze and custom-lacquered wood."

Miles Redd: "I once worked on a magnificent house in Palm Beach that had dining room walls encrusted with nacreous shells laid out in a Chinese pattern."

Alessandra Branca: "I designed a most unusual tent for a dressing room." *My kids would love to have a campout in their closets!*

Travis Smith: "I bought a beautiful and expensive antique canoe and turned it into a dining room china cabinet for one client. For a continental nightclub, I bought over a hundred vintage 1960s "spaghetti" lights from all over the country on eBay, and had them installed along the front windows of the club for an unforgettable lighting statement. For Buffalo Billiards in D.C., I hired a professional theater set designer to create real-looking log trunks that acted as the pool table lights." *This I have to see!*

Willis Watts: "One of my favorite over-the-top touches is using Donghia's mohair fabrics."

Steven Volpe: "My clients and I decided that their dining room would have rich chocolate-brown lacquered walls. It's a beautifully proportioned room that would have an antique French crystal chandelier, fine 18th-century French tables and chairs, and an elegant antique dining table, so the walls had to be distinctive and rich looking. I worked with the painters for several weeks to accomplish exactly the perfect shade of caffè latte for the walls. To get the precise depth and richness I wanted, we had to paint and buff *twelve* layers of paint. The room had to be swathed and enclosed so it would dry without cracking, and dry slowly without attracting dust. Finally, after so much planning, care, and months of meticulous painting, we unveiled the room. It is perfect. The walls glow, especially in candlelight. They are magical. It was worth the work, anxiety, and all the waiting. My clients love this room. It is so elegant and unique."

Is It Worth It to Hire a Designer?

I loved interviewing these designers, who I felt were surprisingly approachable and versatile. But many designers, including the ones mentioned here, can get caught up with expensive jobs where money is no object, forgetting the small and inexpensive touches that can be most memorable in a home.

People who have used designers have told me that the type of designer they most appreciate is the one who encourages them to perform some decorating projects on their own, or the one who finds that diamond in the rough that saves the client a considerable amount of money. Nobody wants to pick up a piece that they love on a trip, in a store, or at a flea market, only to be yelled at by a designer who feels the client has overstepped his or her bounds. However, my experience has taught me that such designers are the unfortunate exception rather than the rule; most designers I have met over the years prefer working with informed clients with a feel for their own personal styles.

Gone are the days when designers can get away with buying all of the furniture for a house from a design center. Today's consumers are savvier, and generally want to buy pieces gradually through a variety of sources. I recently met the president of one of the best-known high-end furniture companies in America. When I asked her where she buys her own furniture, she told me, "I don't feel like waiting twelve to sixteen weeks for my furniture to be delivered, so I just go to IKEA. Besides, I find the shopping experience at places like IKEA to be fun and not so serious." Even the bigwigs love a bargain!

In my opinion, a conscientious designer continually expands his or her knowledge base by seeking out new furnishings sources. In a recent study conducted by the San Francisco Design Center, most designers claimed to know only thirty sources from which to buy furniture. However, many of these designers are probably tempted to stick with just a few of these sources, simply because it is easier to do so. When interviewing a prospective designer, don't be bashful inquiring about their sources—that's the only way you'll get a feel for how wide the designer is willing to cast his or her net in seeking out items for your project. To accommodate the expanding furniture industry, the best designers will break out from their usual shopping patterns. Today's most creative designers feel they must travel to find new and untapped sources, and the most up-to-date designers have embraced online shopping just like the rest of us.

To the Designers: Thanks for All the Wonderful Tips!

To each of the designers who agreed to be interviewed for this book, I offer my thanks for sharing your thoughts, sources, and creativity.

As I mentioned at the beginning of this chapter, we've all had dreams of redoing our homes. Hopefully this brief time spent as a "fly on the wall" of the nation's experts has not only inspired you to tackle such a project, but has also given you some useful tips to make your redecorating dreams come true.

Up-and-Comers

North America's
Ten Best
Newly-Discovered
Furniture Designers

Today's furniture shoppers are more inclined to buy furniture made by well-known designers whose names they have heard than pieces made by unknown artists. It saddens me to realize that designer names mean so much in this industry, because careful examination of many well-known "designer" pieces often reveals that they are no higher in quality than pieces made by lesser-known designers. Moreover, many famous designers do not even design their own pieces, and behind-the-scenes designers never get recognized for creating these famous-name designs.

I spend much of my time examining the designs of the newest and hottest furniture designers in North America, and I recognize that many of these designers will become household names in the furniture industry during the next few years. So I've decided to unveil the country's best untapped resources for fine furniture. I looked all over the country to find the best representations of outstanding furniture design in North America today. Many of these names may be unrecognizable to you, but I believe that these designers will go far in the furniture design world.

In my research for this chapter, I tried to find different types of artists. As a result, no two artists profiled in this book design the same kind of furniture for the same purpose. Some of these designers are high-end contemporary; some are excellent wood craftsmen; some are great designers of low-priced, fun furniture. I even selected a woman who is designing 18th-century-style French garden furniture using branches—and yes, I mean branches from trees! Each designer has had different kinds of schooling, and some were never formally trained at all. Some work with only one kind of material, and others work with a variety. Some are concerned with using only organic materials, while others use the skins of dead animals to cover their pieces. The one thing they all have in common, as I discovered when I called each of them to tell them that I wanted to include them in my book, is that they are all passionate about their art. Just like inventors, which they really are, these artists feel that their designs serve a certain purpose—whether utilitarian, economic, or aesthetic.

In this chapter, I have listed the artists alphabetically. Under each artist's caption, I have included a Web site, if available, as well as an address, E-mail address, and phone number. This information will allow you to access the work of this wonderful and talented bunch. In addition, I will constantly update this list of designers on my Web site, because I want you to have the best choices possible for selecting well-designed furniture at reasonable prices.

Amy Allison

Contact Information
Troscan Design
2000 West Fulton,
Suite F319
Chicago, IL 60612
(312) 733-0158
www.troscandesign.com;
amy@troscandesign.com

Biography

Amy Allison, originally from Michigan, is the Senior Designer at Troscan Design in Chicago, Illinois. Amy's background consists of having designed furniture pieces for famous furniture designers, including Christian Liagre and Holly Hunt. Amy is a graduate of Adrian College in Adrian, Michigan and Kendall College of Art & Design in Grand Rapids, Michigan.

Inspiration

Amy strives to create modern, simple, and graceful furniture. She believes in pure forms with clean lines that are built with the highest attention to detail and materials. She has been inspired by designers like Ted Muehling and Charles and Ray Eames. A multi-talented artist, Amy enjoys designing hardware, lighting, and accessories in addition to furniture.

I selected Amy for inclusion in this book because I think she is one of the most talented and creative sketch designers I have met. In a time when computers have largely replaced handwork, Amy has remained true to her skill and passion. The School of the Art Institute of Chicago, where Amy has taken classes, praised Amy as one of the most talented furniture sketchers with whom it has worked. Amy's talent has also been recognized by some of the most well-respected furniture designers in the world.

Tyler Hays for BDDW

Contact Information
BDDW
5 Crosby Street
New York, NY 10013
(212) 625-1215
www.bddw.com
info@bddw.com

Biography

Raised in a cabin in Oregon, Tyler Hays founded his furniture company in 1994. Tyler is a graduate of the University of Oregon with a Fine Arts degree. He began his career as a painter and sculptor. Today, his A-list clientele come to him for his unusual furniture, paintings, and sculptures. His furniture has been recognized for its quiet and simple forms and materials and impeccable craftsmanship. Some have compared his wood designs to those of George Nakashima, the original master of the organic use of natural elements of tree shapes in furniture.

Inspiration

"I don't really think of myself as a furniture designer—it's more of an aesthetic or a process, and I have hired several people with the same ideals," says Hays. Although he claims not to be inspired by any furniture styles of the past, Tyler collects beat-up antiques and likes them better the more they age. He says that if a piece looks better with age, the designer has created a successful piece of furniture. Each piece he designs is handcrafted in his company's 10,000-square-foot workshop in Williamsburg, Brooklyn by a staff of artisans and engineers. Joshua Vogel, Tyler's longtime business partner, architect, and master craftsman, oversees the Brooklyn workshop, which is equipped with full production machinery for work in wood, metal, ceramic, and stone. The company's 4,000-square-foot showroom, located on a quiet cobblestone street in New York's Soho neighborhood, is serene and unimposing, with brick arches and a gigantic skylight.

I was drawn to Tyler's strong sense of design—and, in particular, his skill in woodworking, the likes of which I have almost never seen before when I walked through one of the world's tallest front doors, a creation that he designed entirely by hand. Tyler creates wood designs that could easily fit into a rustic chateau, but that are also forward-thinking and chic. I am especially impressed with his cabinets, which feature exposed wood fronts encased in contrasting lacquered frames that highlight the luscious grains of his woods. The frame colors stand out, and draw your eye to the unusual craftsmanship of the frames and the doors of the cabinets. Tyler's wood pieces do not have a flat feel to them; they are delicately carved with subtle curves and angles. His work has a certain feeling of "humility" that I think sets Tyler and his process apart from much of the contemporary design scene. He is also one of the most humble designers I know.

Noleen Kutash for Phases Africa

Contact Information
Phases Africa at The Collection
315 South Roberson Boulevard
Los Angeles, CA 90048
(949) 721-9661
www.phasesafrica.com
Noleen@creativedetailing.com

Biography

Growing up in wine country near Cape Town, South Africa, Noleen Kutash spent her youth experiencing the beauty and spirit of the African landscape, and the mixture of her homeland's traditional tribal culture with its European heritage. Keen for adventure, Noleen joined South African Airways as a flight attendant. On one of the airline's flights, she met and fell in love with her future husband, an American producer of musicals. In 1984, she made her home in the United States.

In the process of observing her husband's theater productions take shape, Noleen became his "creative detailer." Given her natural flair for costume design, Noleen decided to purchase a theatrical wardrobe storehouse. With an entrepreneurial spirit and a bold eye for style, she formed her own business called Creative Detailing, which created costumes for regional theater productions across the U.S.

In 2000, Noleen spent a year in Florence studying the best in European design, both traditional and contemporary. In 2001 she traveled to Africa, and returned to the United States with a small range of home furnishing products. These products were quickly snapped up by leading retail stores such as Fred Segal and Thomas Schoos. Recognizing a void in the U.S. market for sophisticated home furnishings with a distinctly African character, Noleen opened her showroom in Los Angeles in 2004.

Inspiration
During years spent living in the United States, Noleen has returned regularly to visit her African

homeland. Since the end of apartheid in 1990, she has witnessed the development of an innovative, contemporary design scene in South Africa, and has been inspired by the ways in which modern design has been applied to traditional artistry, opening up a new international market and reestablishing the cultural pride and economic status of wonderfully skilled tribal craftspeople. Noleen's goal with the Phases Africa line is to combine a passionate interest in contemporary design with a pride in her African cultural heritage. She travels widely in South Africa and across the African continent to source her stylish and unique range of products directly from designers, artists, and local craftspeople.

As I searched the country for designers offering something different, I found Noleen and her most unusual collection. What fascinated me most about Noleen was her ability to take the European influences that came to Africa after World War II and implement them in her furniture designs. Her furniture does not reflect a traditional tribal style. Her pieces are interesting to look at and make great conversation pieces (how about the ostrich egg chandelier made from real ostrich eggs!). Her designs are contemporary in feel, but borrow from traditional concepts.

The Design Team for Maine Cottage Furniture

Contact Information
Maine Cottage Furniture
P.O. Box 935
247 Portland Street, Bldg. C
Yarmouth, ME 04096
(888) 859-5522
www.mainecottage.com
info@mainecottage.com

Biography

Maine Cottage Furniture was founded in 1988 by Carol and Peter Bass. Carol Bass got the idea for the company's designs when she saw photo stylists painting found cottage furniture to add color to presentations in home-decorating magazines. Peter Bass saw themes in the fashion business that he thought could translate into the furniture business—color, and lots of it, used to design casual home furnishings that would appeal to consumers who grew up with color magazines, TV, and movies.

Inspiration

The design team at Maine Cottage presents their products in the context of a coastal home. Carol Bass designed simple architectural wood furniture painted in colors from elements found in seasonal cottages in Maine. The company's customers—a rapidly expanding group—use its products to furnish their homes in a colorful, casual style.

Maine Cottage has tuned its business practices—including design, merchandising, sales, and customer service—to consumers who want their homes to look great but would like to avoid turning a decorating project into their life's work. By creating recommended color combinations and employing a disciplined approach to product development, consumers can choose freely from the company's collection of products.

The goal at Maine Cottage is to help the customer easily choose an exciting collection of products that go together without seeming "matchy-matchy," and without restricting the customer to buying products in "suites." Along with the painted wood furniture for which it is known, Maine Cottage also offers a nice selection of upholstered pieces, along with textile prod-

ucts such as bed linens, quilts, rugs, and fabrics (over 120 fabric choices). Maine Cottage has two company-owned stores, and plans to open three additional showrooms in the next two years. The company offers its products in 100 retail stores around the country.

Maine Cottage was an easy choice for me. I increasingly see Maine Cottage's furniture mixed with all kinds of décor at furniture stores around the country, and I love it in every setting. Maine Cottage, a company virtually unknown until the past few years, has revolutionized the way we think about cottage-style furniture. It has designed furniture that is traditional, but makes a bold, contemporary statement with color and shape. Maine Cottage's creative design team has designed cottage-style furniture in a variety of luscious colors—forty in all, including shrimp, ochre, china green, mango, and tomato, just to whet your appetite. The quality of its construction is as outstanding as its color options.

Daniel Michalik

Contact Information
Daniel Michalik
253 Knight Street, #2
Providence, RI 02909
(401) 952-5579
www.danielmichalik.com;
danielmichalik@mac.com

Biography
Daniel Michalik is from Providence, Rhode Island. He recently completed the Master's Program at the Rhode Island School of Design in the Department of Furniture Design. Daniel is currently managing studios and

teaching at Brown University, as well as running his own design/build firm, where he creates furniture using underutilized, overlooked, environmentally responsible materials. His most recent explorations have involved uncovering the vast potential of cork to perform in ways that no other material can. While he produces most of his work himself, he is also developing new products for international manufacturers. He has exhibited internationally, including at the Milan Furniture Fair 2004, and at the NeoCon Chicago World's Trade Fair 2004, and has been featured in such publications as *Wallpaper*, *UKMetro*, *American Craft*, and the *Boston Globe*.

Inspiration

Daniel's work focuses on researching and expanding the uses of underutilized, unconventional materials. His objective is to investigate new materials that could lead to creating innovative methods of production and new ways of interacting with the environment. His recent work taps the rich potential of

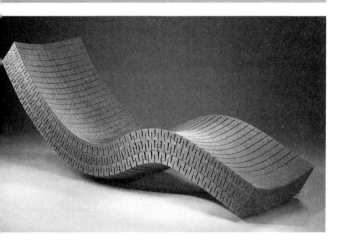

cork, an engaging and environmentally responsible material. Daniel enjoys working with cork because cork is completely sustainable, regenerating itself every ten years for harvest. It is also recyclable, plentiful, and wonderfully tactile. The material he uses originates as the waste material from the wine-stopper industry. Through this series of objects, he has tried to explore the deep potential of the material, making it do things it has never before done, as well as things that only cork can do.

Daniel's work is interesting to me on a few different levels. First, as a specialist within a narrow area of the furniture industry, he has spent an incredible amount of time getting to know how cork works, and he has truly perfected the many ways furniture can be made using cork. He has become one of the world's most knowledgeable cork furniture designers, and has come up with several sophisticated techniques for molding and layering his pieces. His designs are chic and transitional in style, but work well with a classic décor. I also like the fact that cork is recyclable, and that using cork means not killing a perfectly healthy tree. Cork is an en-

vironmentally good choice when selecting organic furniture. I also find Daniel's cork designs to be softer and more comfortable than many kinds of wood seating.

Anne-Marie Midy and Jorge Almada for Casamidy

Contact Information
Casamidy
Hospicio 2
San Miguel de Allende
GTO 37700, Mexico
52-415-152-0403
www.casamidy.com;
casamidy@casamidy.com

Biography

Casamidy, a Mexican furniture and interior design company, was started in 1998 by the husband-and-wife team of Anne-Marie Midy and Jorge Almada. Trained at the Rhode Island School of Design, Anne-Marie Midy became an art director at *Martha Stewart Living*. Jorge Almada previously worked for Portico under Stephen Werther, when it was one of the most influential retail furniture concepts in the U.S. Jorge studied at Parsons School of Design in New York.

The couple moved to Mexico from New York in 1999. They have been featured in *House & Garden*, which named Anne-Marie as one of its "50 New Tastemakers," as well as *World of Interiors*—in which they were the first Mexican contemporary designers ever to be featured—and *Elle Décor*. Casamidy's clients include Rockwell Group, KWID, Ian Schrager Hotels, and W Hotels.

Inspiration

Midy and Almada's aspiration has been to fuse design ideas with traditional artisan resources largely

neglected in Mexico. They aim to make their designs contemporary, yet infused with a cultural value stemming from the way in which each piece is crafted.

I chose this design team because I loved their modern-day interpretations of serious French antiques. I like their idea of taking traditional French-style furniture and updating its look in a not-so-serious way. The result is sophisticated and chic. Although their chairs are made from steel, they don't look heavy or clumsy. They have also used colorful and unusual fabrics to make cushions. Midy and Almada have been influenced by European furniture design, and it shows in their designs, which include traces of the past. The furniture has a sophisticated European flair, yet reflects the casual and rustic look of Mexico. The combination is fabulous.

Richard Shapiro for StudioLo

Contact Information
Richard Shapiro
8905 Melrose Avenue
Los Angeles, CA 90069
(310) 275-6700
www.rshapiroantiques.com
Richard@rshapiroantiques.com

Biography
After thirty years as a student and collector of postwar contemporary art and period furniture, Richard Shapiro's establishment of Richard Shapiro Antiques and Works of Art was a natural progression. An ele-

gant and classic space designed by Shapiro himself, the gallery serves as a backdrop for the many rare and special pieces displayed there. The antiques gallery has an adjoining garden and motor court that is reminiscent of an age-old European town house.

While Shapiro's gallery features some of the world's finest antiques, he has also recently launched a line of French 1940s-inspired furniture called StudioLo. This furniture line has been designed to complement the gallery's period furniture. During Shapiro's thirty-year business life, he co-founded and designed both the architecture and interiors for the Grill restaurants in Beverly Hills, Chicago, and San José. He served for many years as a trustee at the Museum of Contemporary Art, where he was the inaugural Chairman of MOCA's Drawing Committee.

Inspiration

Shapiro's clean-lined, minimal pieces are intended to produce striking juxtapositions when paired with the more complex antique objects. Shapiro views his gallery as a salon as much as a place of business. He is

happiest describing his collection with interested visitors, be they clients or simply people who want to take in the ambience and perhaps recharge their aesthetic batteries.

I fell in love with Richard's antiques gallery when I was in Los Angeles. I didn't even know about his StudioLo line at that time. When I visited his Web site to learn more about his business, I was amazed to find such wonderful, simple, and elegant French forties-inspired furniture. I researched his entire line, and there was not one piece I didn't want for myself! I especially like the fact that Richard's line features a wide variety of colors, bold and subtle, and unusual shapes and curves in every piece. Few have been able to reproduce the look of this era as well as Richard Shapiro.

Laura Spector for Laura Spector Rustic Design

Contact Information
Laura Spector Rustic Design
786 Westport Turnpike
Fairfield, CT 06430
(203) 254-3952
www.lauraspectorrusticdesign.com;
lsrustic@aol.com

Biography

Based in Fairfield, Connecticut, Laura Spector is a designer and builder of rustic furnishings. She creates whimsical, one-of-a-kind furnishings in the 18th-century European Romantic tradition. Laura uses branches and ironwork to design this sculptural furniture, much of which can be used both inside and outside the home. Laura's work has captured the attention of experts in the antique garden furniture field, such as Barbara Israel, who has described Laura

as "the only contemporary artist working in this medium. She has mastered the technique of the uninterrupted line, creating works of classical symmetry from natural forms."

Laura has been featured in the *New York Times*, *House & Garden*, *Interior Design*, *O: The Oprah Magazine*, and *Architectural Design*, as well as several books on rustic and garden design. She has received commissions from Bergdorf Goodman, Macy's, Catherine Malendrino, Mario Testino, and Dallas's new W Hotel.

Inspiration

Laura is inspired by nature and the look of 18th-century French gardens. In her own words, she likes to "blur the line between rustic and refined, and is always amazed at how easily my material lends itself to that exchange." Laura spends much of her time in the woods near her Connecticut home, observing nature and carefully studying tree branches and how they move. She carries over the branches' natural forms into her furniture designs. Laura admits that she never preconceives a design; rather, the designs come to her while she is in the throes of creating a piece with her

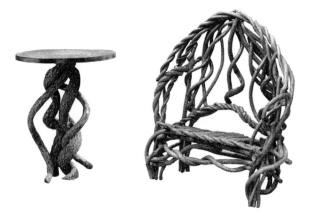

own two hands. Laura is self-taught in the art of working with natural elements to design furniture.

Sometimes when I go furniture shopping, I want to find something different but I don't know what. I like finding pieces that really have no name or genre, and sometimes no purpose besides simply being fun to look at. For me, Laura's designs are just that: fun. Her furniture is more like a piece of sculpture, yet so inviting that you want to feel what it's like to try out her beds or feel what it is like to sit in one of her chairs—or even rest a drink on one of her side tables. I saw pictures of Laura's work, and I knew there was something very special about her designs. In a subtle and romantic way, Laura's designs look like they belong in a medieval garden.

Peter Tielmann for EQ3

Contact Information
EQ3
70 Lexington Park
Winnipeg, Manitoba
Canada R2G 4H2
(204) 954-7070
www.eq3.com;
info@eq3.com

Biography

EQ3, founded in 2001, is a division of Palliser Furniture of Winnepeg, Canada. As President of EQ3, Peter Tielmann has had an impressive career for such a young guy—he's only thirty-five! Tielmann was born in Russia as the youngest of eight children. His family was German, and was held as prisoners of war by the Russian regime. Eventually, Tielmann and his family were allowed to return to Germany. Peter studied architecture, and received the U.S. equivalent of an MBA in Germany. He not only continued to study both in Lithuania and Canada, but also began a business with a friend importing health-care-related electronic equipment from Taiwan and China. In 1998, he left his business and came to Palliser Furniture, the parent of EQ3—Canada's largest manufacturer of assembled household furniture.

EQ3 has fourteen stores across North America. In the U.S., EQ3 stores have opened in San Francisco, Los Angeles, Grand Rapids, Richmond, and Charlotte. In the coming years, EQ3 is likely to move into Europe, Latin America, and Asia.

Inspiration

Tielmann and the entire design team at EQ3 approach furniture design as having a global appeal. They believe that style watchers around the world are keenly aware of what hip furniture design looks like, especially leading-edge European design. But, as in the fashion industry, the best furniture designs are often unaffordable to the average consumer. EQ3 is furniture as fashion. The team's goal is to design quality designs that are innovative but not expensive.

Art DeFehr, CEO and President of Palliser, says this about EQ3's mission:

> Over the years, we've always viewed ourselves as a sort of bridge between North America and Europe, so our products have always had a stronger contemporary flavor. But EQ3 takes a whole step forward into a style range the traditional retailer doesn't even touch. It's more fun and more functional.

I first saw EQ3's designs at the High Point, North Carolina Market last year. I was immediately drawn to the line, which seemed more progressive than that of other manufacturers I had viewed. I love EQ3's wide array of hip styles, colorful fabrics, and low prices. The furniture and the company's image remind me of IKEA, but the selection is easier to peruse and the staff, young and fashionable, are well-versed in the inventory and fabric options. EQ3 has furniture for virtually every room in a house, and the pieces are not only stylish but also well-made for the money. I believe that EQ3 will be a huge success in the U.S. and around the world.

Steven Volpe for Hedge and Steven Volpe Designs

Contact Information
Hedge Gallery
48 Gold Street
San Francisco, CA 94133
(415) 357-1102
www.hedgegallery.com;
www.stevenvolpe.com
info@hedgegallery.com

Biography

Steven Volpe has been designing residential interiors for fifteen years. After being schooled in Northern California, he moved to San Francisco to work with designers Anthony Hail, Eleanor Ford, and Tony Machado. Subsequently he spent three years in Paris working with the American architect Bronner Schaul. In 1988, he returned to California to work on an apartment in the Brocklebank on Nob Hill in San Francisco. Since then, his small firm has grown to eight, and is currently working on fifteen residential and commercial projects, ranging from modern to classic. Mr. Volpe's latest endeavor is Hedge, a furniture gallery and manufacturing company he founded with business partner, Roth Martin, two years ago.

Inspiration

In partnership with Roth Martin, Steven Volpe created Hedge, a company that designs and produces a distinctive collection of furniture inspired by mid-20th-century artists and designers. Hedge takes the best of past construction, reinterprets innovative design and fashion, and then adds fresh uses of metals, colored lacquer, luxurious leathers, and various woods and finishes to create future collectibles of quality and style.

In terms of furniture trends, Hedge's belief is that furniture is manufactured in multiples, but each piece has an individual identity and can be used in a variety of functions.

Steven's designs are wonderfully classic and simple, but have an edge that is all his. The shapes, proportions, and colors are what caught my eye when I visited his small shop in San Francisco. I also love the fact that Steven has beautifully blended his own-designed furniture pieces with the vintage pieces at Hedge.

8

Name That Furniture

The Details Behind
History's Most
Famous Pieces

I n your everyday lives, you see furniture everywhere. And if my hunch is correct, I'll bet that sometimes you forget what certain types of pieces are called! I can't tell you how many times people have asked me, "What do you call that chair again? I forget ..."

So, here it is: I've compiled a list of some of the most well-known pieces of furniture ever made. Now you can learn a little something about the furniture you have seen over and over again through the years—and you'll never again forget what to call it.

Chaise Lounge

16th century, France

Also called a chaise longue

Designed for people to lie on their backs, not on their sides

Caned seat

Secretary

William and Mary period, late 17th century, England

Front drops down for writing purposes

Highboy

William and Mary period, England, late 17th century

Used for additional storage anywhere in a house

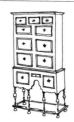

Gateleg Table

England, 1670

Made during reign of Charles II

Designed for utility; table can be folded

Winged-Back Chair

England, 17th century

Jacobean period

First upholstered chair, and probably the first comfortable chair

Wings on chair designed to block drafts

Windsor Chair

England, 17th century

Designed to be durable; not necessarily comfortable

Turned spindles, wooden seat

Queen Anne Chair

England, early 18th century

Commissioned by Queen Anne

Designed by many different cabinetmakers of the time

Designed to be comfortable, elegant, and lightweight

Chippendale Chair

England, 18th century

Designed by Thomas
Chippendale and other
cabinetmakers of the era

Influenced by Chinese,
Gothic, and mid-18th-century
French styles

Mahogany wood

Library Table

18th century, England

Designed during reign of
George I

Designed to have two banks,
with two to four drawers in each,
and usually on a pedestal base

Commode

France, early 18th century

Designed by André-Charles
Boulle for Louis XIV

Highly ornamented, served as a
focal point of the room in which
it was featured

Louis XV Armchair

France, mid-18th century

Designed to be comfortable to
the back: curved, light, and
elegant

Reflected the luxurious court life

Biedermeier Chair

Produced from 1810 to 1835, primarily in Austria and Germany

The name "Biedermeier" is attributed to a satirical cartoon, popular in early 19th-century Europe, depicting a wealthy man surrounded by folk-style furniture

Popular designers include Josef Danhauser, Karl Friedrich Schinkel, Josef Hiltl

Chesterfield Sofa—aka English Library Sofa

Designed in 1880 in Victorian-era England

Unknown designer

First fully upholstered settee

Name derives from either a Derbyshire town or one of the Earls of Chesterfield

Brass casters for easy moving

B3 Wassily Chair

Germany, 1925

Designed by Marcel Breuer

Inspired by the handlebars of a bike; made from tubular steel

Designed to be inexpensive, comfortable, attractive, and mass-produced

Barcelona Chair

Germany, 1929

Designed by
Mies van der Rohe

One of the first designers to
work with steel in furniture
design

Eames Plywood Chair

America, 1946

Designed by Ray and Charles
Eames

Designed to be affordable, yet
high quality

First molded plywood chair that
didn't require a cushion and
could be mass-produced

DAR Chair

America, 1948

Designed by Ray and Charles
Eames for Herman Miller

Plastic form emphasizing
ergonomics and technological
advancements

Bertoia Chair

America, 1952

Designed by Harry Bertoia

Designed to be flexible, with an
easy-to-move body

Egg Chair

Denmark, 1957

Designed by Arne Jacobsen for
Fritz Hansen

Simple form typical of Danish
furniture

Pivoting chair with wool or
leather upholstery over a plastic
molded shell and steel pedestal

Tulip Chair

America, 1957

Designed by Eero Saarinen, a
Finnish designer

The goal of the piece was to
simplify the leg; its base is a
single pedestal

9

Not a Conclusion, But a Beginning...

have written *The Best Furniture Buying Tips Ever!* to help you navigate your way in and out of furniture stores, and to help you become a savvy shopper. So let's summarize the information provided in this portable guide—information that will get you started on one of the most exciting adventures of your life: creating a home that serves your needs, reflects your personality, and ultimately establishes your personal lifestyle.

In this book, I have examined the entire furniture industry from the viewpoints of consumers, retailers, furniture designers, and interior designers, drawing upon my own experiences as a consumer, retailer, and reviewer of furniture and furniture stores. The best education I have received in this industry has been from hearing other people's stories and opinions—and not from coffee table books, which are filled with pretty pictures, but not with the information consumers really need. This is why I have sought out and attempted to share the experiences and opinions of the many types of people currently working in this vast furniture industry. My hope is that by learning from others' experiences, you can avoid some of furniture shopping's pitfalls and focus instead on its joys.

You now have clear guidelines on what to look for when buying furniture—from upholstered goods to case goods, organic furniture to antiques.

Moreover, to take the guesswork out of remembering important dates in the history of furniture, you can now recall some of the great and entertaining stories about the royals and their influences on furniture styles—not to mention some of their extracurricular activities!

In addition, you've been provided with an entire chapter on twenty of the most popular pieces of furniture ever made—pieces that you probably recognize, but about which you may not remember names or details. When they were first produced, most of these pieces were considered on the cutting edge of both technology and design. Knowing about them will definitely enhance your furniture IQ!

To help you make better-informed and more-satisfying decisions when buying furniture, this book also includes a basic glossary of terms, line drawings of furniture styles, and a reference resource. I also invite you to check my Web site for a directory of over 500 other furniture Web sites.

I have also interviewed some of the nation's most respected interior designers in order to gather their thoughts on the furniture industry. These top designers have shared with you some of their favorite resources for furniture and accessories.

And finally, none of us would have any furniture if we didn't have some really talented furniture designers—professionals whose jobs are not only to design furniture, but also to constantly think about what our furniture needs will or should be. Unfortunately, many of the most talented furniture designers never get mentioned in major publications. For this reason, I examined the work of many artists and selected the ten individuals who I believe are today's best up-and-coming furniture designers. Get to know them now—and when they're famous, brag that you heard about them here first!

One final reminder: Throughout this book I have "red-flagged" the information you should review before each shopping trip—even if you take this book with you when you shop. It never hurts to review the tricks of the trade before you leave the house—after all, you never know when you might need them!

With all of this in mind, I feel confident that you are now ready to embark on your furniture-shopping adventure! But you don't have to do it alone. I would be happy to answer any questions you may have on my Web site at *www.jenniferlitwin.com*. I'll make every attempt to respond to your questions personally and correctly. I look forward to hearing your thoughts and concerns, and sharing your furniture-shopping adventures. Best of luck!

Glossary

Antiques Restorer
An individual who returns an antique piece of furniture to its original condition. Sometimes known as a "conservationist."

Arts and Crafts
Also known as "Mission Style," a reference to styles seen in California missions. A movement that began in England in the early 1900s, characterized by straight lines, oak wood, airy and rustic looks, exposed hardware, functional designs, minimal ornamentation, brass tacks, and leather. Famous Designers include William Morris, Gustav Stickley, and Roycroft Industries.

American Empire
The period in the 1800s during which America came into its own in terms of furniture design. This period was filled with experimentation and revivals.

American Federal
A period lasting from the late 1700s to mid-1800s. Pieces from this period include American Empire pieces, which were inspired by French Empire furniture but were heavier and larger in size. Pieces feature straight legs, and the fronts of cabinets and chairs are typically curved. Mahogany was commonly used. A well-known designer from this period is Duncan Phyfe.

Art Deco
A period lasting from 1908 to 1930. Typical pieces include seated furniture with shorter legs. Pieces typically feature luxurious fabrics made from silk and exotic woods such as ebony, amboyna, and pallisander. Steel, leather, and glass were introduced during this period. Enamel and mother-of-pearl were also popular materials. Pieces generally display a sophisticated style.

Famous designers from this period include Le Corbusier, Pierre Chareau, Louis Majorelle, and Jacques Émile Ruhlmann.

Art Moderne
A period lasting from 1925 to 1940. Pieces from this period are similar in style to Art Deco pieces, but their designs are more extreme and angular. Pieces often incorporate the designs of international designers, and mark the transition of Art Deco style into the mid-20th-century.

Barcelona Chair
A mid-20th-century chair designed by Mies van der Rohe, made from steel and leather.

Biedermeier
Refers to furniture designed in Austria and Germany between 1815 and 1830. Pieces display a folk style that constitutes a rejection of previous European styles. Typical features include simple lines, functional designs, tapered or straight legs, an emphasis on wood grains, and contemporary styling. Common woods include maple, birch, ash, or fruitwood. Many Biedermeier pieces were reproduced by the Swedes in the late 1800s. Famous designers of the period include Josef Danhauser and Karl Friedrich Schinkel.

Biedermeier Chair
A style of chair modeled after French Empire styles. See "Biedermeier" above.

Bertoia Chair
A mid-20th-century chair designed by Harry Bertoia, made from woven steel.

Blocks
Simple rectangular pieces of wood glued on furniture frames at various stress points, such as the corners of sofas, to add strength to a piece.

Bottom of the Hide
Refers to the area farthest below the fur of an animal that is processed into leather. This bottom-grain

leather is softer and less durable than top-grain leather. Suede comes from the bottom of the hide.

Cabriole Legs
"S"-curved furniture legs used in 18th- and early-19th-century designs.

Case Goods
Non-upholstered pieces of furniture made of wood, such as chests, tables, and cabinetry.

Chaise Lounge
A reclining chair with a seat long enough to support the outstretched legs of the sitter. Also referred to by its French name, a chaise longue.

Chesterfield Sofa
A large, overstuffed sofa with upright armrests. Named after the 19th-century Earl of Chesterfield.

Chippendale Furniture
Furniture produced between 1755 and 1790 in a style very popular in both England and the United States. Designed by Thomas Chippendale. Pieces typically display considerable use of carving, as well as claw-and-ball feet. Heavily influenced by Chinese design.

Chippendale Chair
See "Chippendale Furniture" above. Chair characterized by a wooden back that is pierced, with designs cut into it. Typically features claw-and-ball feet and upholstered seats.

Colonial
Refers to the Colonial era of North American history, which lasted from the 1600s to the mid-1700s. In terms of furniture, this period began with simple and practical furniture, such as chests and trestle tables in English styles, and cedar and pine furniture made in New Jersey, New York, and Pennsylvania. Later styles are more ornate and resemble Queen Anne, Chippendale, and French designs, including Windsor chairs.

Commode

A low cabinet or chest of drawers, often elaborately decorated and usually on legs or short feet. 18th-century English.

Cross-Grain Woods

Woods cut across the grain. Cross-grain woods tend to be weaker than solid woods.

Foam

Synthetic material used as a filling in upholstered furniture.

French Empire

A period lasting from 1804 to 1815, during the reign of Napoleon and his wife, Josephine. Characterized by Asian-influenced designs that incorporated Egyptian and Greek motifs. Pieces feature fancy but simple lines. Typical features include marble tabletops, metal feet, mahogany and rosewood construction, and motifs signifying the empire: lions, sphinxes, eagles, and "N"s. Famous designers from this period include Charles Percier and Pierre Fontaine.

French Provincial

A period lasting from the late 1600s to the 1800s. Characterized by furniture made in the French provinces. Pieces typically have a rustic, less-expensive look, and are built from local woods such as walnut and pine. Some designs imitate those made in cities for aristocrats. Popular styles include Windsor and ladder-back chairs.

Furniture Guilds

Guilds achieved their peak influence in the mid-18th century in France and England. They were associations of individuals who designed furniture, usually with a monarch's authorization or commission.

Gateleg Table

A drop-leaf table with movable legs arranged in pairs.

Georgian Period

A period encompassing most of the 18th century after 1715—the reigns of the three King Georges. Pieces from this period are typically made from mahogany, and feature cabriole legs and claw-and-ball feet. Rich upholstery was introduced during this period, as was the sideboard. Famous designers of the period include Chippendale, Adam, and Hepplewhite and Sheraton.

Gilding

Gold leafing, or a paint simulating gold applied to wood furniture.

Hardwoods

Wood from deciduous trees such as oak, cherry, and maple.

Highboy

Associated with the William and Mary period in the early 1700s, the highboy is a chest on top of another chest with legs.

Josephine

Wife of Napoleon Bonaparte of France, she influenced the style of French furniture during the early 1800s.

Joint

The point at which two pieces of wood furniture are joined. Blocks, screws, mortise/tenon, and glue are all used to join furniture segments.

Kiln-Dried Hardwood

Hardwood that has been dried in a kiln to resist warping or weakening. Oak, maple, and birch are usually kiln-dried.

Louis XIII

Refers to a period encompassing the first half of the 17th century, during the reign of France's Louis XIII. During this period, furniture guilds designed furniture with the help of the monarchs. Pieces from this period typically feature twisted legs, cabinets divided into two parts, and fancy carvings.

Louis XIV
Refers to a period lasting from 1643 to 1715, during the reign of France's Louis XIV. Also known as the Baroque period. During this period, furniture guilds designed furniture with the input of the monarch. Typical pieces include tables and chairs with straight legs, high-back chairs, pieces made from carved oak and walnut, upholstered pieces, marble-top console tables, and pieces featuring gilding.

Louis XV
Refers to a period lasting from 1715 to 1774, during the reign of France's Louis XV. Also known as the Rococo period. Characterized by fancy, ornate furniture with a feminine style, and featuring many curves and scrollwork. Typical features include bombé chests, cabriole legs, an emphasis on comfort and extensive use of color, and extensive gilding. During this period, guilds controlled the quality and construction of furniture. Famous designers from this period include Louis XV's mistress, Madame de Pompadour, as well as Mathieu Criard and Charles Cressent.

Louis XVI
Refers to a period encompassing the late 18th century in France, during the reign of Louis XVI. Pieces from this period feature rectangular legs, squarish designs, and small scales. Famous designers from this period include Georges Jacob and Jean-Henri Riesener.

Marie Antoinette
Wife of Louis XVI.

Modern Movement (Includes Bauhaus and Retro)
A movement lasting from the early to mid-1900s, characterized by functional furniture made around

the world. Accessories are important in designs of this movement, as are popular designs that fit everyday lives. Plastic, metal, and bentwood are common materials. Famous designers include Bertoia, Marcel Breuer, Le Corbusier, Eames, Gio Ponti, Eero Saarinen, and Mies van der Rohe.

Mission
Refers to furniture originally produced between 1895 and 1910 in Southern California. Pieces were typically made from dark-stained oak. Inspired by the Arts and Crafts movement, they typically feature simple designs with block legs, or straight legs with stretchers. Functionality is of paramount important in pieces from this period. Famous designers include Roycroft Industries, Gustav Stickley, and Frank Lloyd Wright.

Napoleon
Emperor of France from 1804 to 1814. His military campaigns in Egypt, Greece, and Italy heavily influenced many furniture styles during the French Directoire and Empire periods.

Particle Board
Consists of chips of wood coated with glue and pressed into a solid sheet. Often used for tabletops, as well as for the tops and sides of chests.

Period Furniture
Furniture that is original to the time it was produced, as opposed to a reproduction.

Provenance
A piece of furniture's place of origin, or a document certifying its ownership.

Queen Anne
Refers to pieces made in the early 1700s, during the reign of Queen Anne. This period is famous for the invention of highboys and the famous Queen Anne

chair. Cupboards were widely produced during this period, and shell motifs were common.

Queen Anne Chair
Graceful wooden curved-back chair with upholstered seat. Features a vase-styled back curved to fit the body and cabriole legs.

Regency
Refers to furniture produced from the late 1700s to early 1800s, during the regency of England's George IV. This period was marked by the continuation of styles from the early 1700s. The furniture resembles that of the French Directoire period (late 1700s) and the French Empire period (early 1800s), though its pieces are often simpler and smaller. Inspired by Chinese and Egyptian motifs, some chairs feature caning as seats, lacquered frames, and exotic designs. Thomas Sheraton was a famous designer of Regency furniture.

Reproduction
An exact copy of an earlier-produced piece of furniture.

Shaker
Refers to handmade furniture, produced from the late 1700s to early 1800s by an American religious group living in small villages along the East Coast, in Ohio, and in Kentucky. Shaker pieces typically feature no decoration, and extreme functionality is of paramount importance. Typical pieces include swivel chairs and stools. Pieces are typically made from pine, and are often said to resemble French Provincial pieces.

Softwood
The wood of a non-deciduous tree, such as cedar or pine.

Solid Wood
Refers to furniture made with solid boards, which may consist of softwood or hardwood lumber.

Synthetic Fabrics

Man-made fabrics such as rayon, nylon, or polyester, used to cover upholstered furniture.

Top-Grain

Refers to the portion of a hide just beneath the fur of an animal that is processed into leather. A stronger and more durable grain than other leather grains.

Upholstered Furniture

Furniture consisting of stuffing, springs, cushioning, and attached fabric.

Veneer

Often made from expensive pieces of wood, veneers are thin layers of surface wood applied to the top of a piece of solid wood or plywood.

Victorian

Refers to a period lasting from 1837 to 1901, during the reign of Queen Victoria. During this period, production of machine-made furniture became possible. Typical features of Victorian furniture include red velvet upholstery, springs in sofas and chairs, heavy frames, mahogany and walnut construction, and horsehair cushions. Pieces resemble French Rococo pieces. Famous designers include Edward William Godwin, William Morris, Augustus Pugin, and Philip Webb.

Windsor Chair

A chair that became popular in the mid-18th century. Inexpensive and easily copied by the common craftsman, the Windsor chair is all wood, with either a curved or straight back with open slats.

William and Mary

Refers to the period encompassing the late 1600s, during the reign of William and Mary. During this period, upholstered furniture appeared for the first time, and walnut replaced oak as the most popular wood. Pieces from this period often feature floral designs carved in the wood. Windsor chairs were popular during this period.

Winged-Back Chair
Sometimes referred to as a "wing chair." An armchair with a high back from which project large, enclosing side pieces.

Bibliography

Books

Algrant, Christine Pevitt. *Madame de Pompadour, Mistress of France*. New York: Grove Press, 2002.

Baker, H.S. *Furniture in the Ancient World: Origins & Evolution*. New York: Macmillan, 1966.

Bernier, Olivier. *Louis the Beloved: The Life of Louis XV*. New York: Doubleday, 1984.

Bishop, Robert, and Patricia Coblentz. *Furniture 1: Prehistoric Through Rococo*. Washington, D.C.: Smithsonian Institution, 1979.

Boger, Louise Ade. *The Complete Guide to Furniture Styles*. Prospect Heights, Illinois: Waveland Press, Inc., 1969.

Cescinsky, Herbert, and George Leland Hunter. *English and American Furniture*. Garden City, New York: Garden City Publishing Company, Inc., 1929.

Crankshaw, Edward. *Maria Theresa*. New York: Penguin Books, 2001.

Cronin, Vincent. *Louis XIV*. London: Collins, 1964.

Darbyshire, Lydia. *Furniture: The Decorative Arts Library*. Hertfordshire, England: Eagle Editions, 1998.

Eisler, Benita. *Byron: Child of Passion, Fool of Fame*. New York: Vintage Books, 2000.

Farquhar, Michael. *Royal Scandals*. New York: Penguin Books, 2001.

Ketchum, William C., Jr. *Furniture 2: Neoclassic to the Present*. Washington, D.C.: Smithsonian Institution, 1979.

Lucie-Smith, Edward. *Furniture: A Concise History*. London: Thames & Hudson Ltd., 2000.

Murray, Venetia. *An Elegant Madness: High Society in Regency England*. New York: Penguin Books, 2000.

Pool, Daniel. *What Jane Austen Ate and Charles Dickens Knew.* New York: Simon & Schuster, 1993.

Ramsey, L.G.G., and Helen Comstock. *Antique Furniture: The Guide for Collectors, Investors and Dealers.* New York: Hawthorne Books, Inc., 1969.

Salomonsky, Verna Cook. *Masterpieces of Furniture.* New York: Dover Publications, Inc., 1953.

Web Sites

www.cilss.org

www.about-antiques.com

www.oldandsold.com/articles04/furniture1.shtml

www.french-antique-furniture.com/chairhistory.html

www.designaddict.com

www.1stdibs.com

www.dwr.com

www.interiordezine.com

www.channel4.com/history

www.historic-uk.com

www.pbs.org/empires/napoleon.com

www.brainyquote.com

www.detnew.com/2002/decorating

www.victorianweb.org

www.magazines.ivillage.com/housebeautiful

www.online.milwaukee.tec.wi.us.com

www.britannica.com

www.frick.org

www.royalty.nu

www.encarta.msn.com

www.frontera.com

www.wisegeek.com

www.modernfurnitureclassics.com

Index

A

Adam, Robert, *81*
Alexandriuk, Kim
    antiques shows advice, *111*
    decorating advice, *105*
    finishing touches by, *112*
Allison, Amy, *119–121*
Almada, Jorge, *132–134*
American Empire style, *95*
American Federal style, *95*
American furniture styles, *94–95*
antiques. *See also* period furniture
    authenticity of, *55–59*
    avoiding rip-offs, *107*
    buy for love, not money, *21–22*
    certificate of authenticity for, *6–7*
    deodorizing, *27–28*
    as investment, *21–22*
    price research, *73*
    vs. reproductions, *25–27*
antiques shows, *111*
Art Deco style, *93*
Art Moderne style, *93*
Art Nouveau style, *92*
Arts and Crafts furniture, *84*
assembly fees, *3*
auctions, *28–30, 104, 107–108*
Austrian furniture style, *96*
authenticity, *6–7, 55–59*

B

B3 Wassily chair, *148*
Barcelona chair, *149*
bargain shopping tips, *100–108*
Bauhaus style, *96–97*
BDDW, *121–123*
Bell, Robin
    couch buying advice, *108*
    decorating advice, *103–104, 105*
Benneman, G., *89*
Bertoia, *97*
Bertoia chair, *149*
Biedermeier style, *96*
Biedermeir chair, *148*
billing arrangements, *13–14*
blocks, *36, 47, 64–65*
Branca, Alessandra
    couch buying advice, *109*
    decorating advice, *105, 106*
    finishing touches by, *113*
brass tacks, *84*

Breuer, Marcel, *97, 148, 161*
Brighton Pavilion, *83*
burl, *46*

C

cabriole legs, *81, 87*
campaign furniture, *92*
Carlton House, *83*
carving, *79–81, 85*
Casamidy, *132–134*
case goods
    composition of, *44–45, 65*
    definition of, *43–44*
    finishes, *48–49*
    joinery, *47–48, 66, 67*
    price factors, *65–67*
    purchasing guidelines, *53*
    types of woods, *45–46*
cedar blocks, *28*
certificate of authenticity, *6–7*
chaise lounge, *145*
Chareau, Pierre, *93*
Chelsea Passage, *105*
Chesterfield sofa, *148*
Chippendale, Thomas, *81*
Chippendale chair, *147*
Chippendale furniture, *81*
Circa Lighting, *106*
Classic Sofa, *104*
claw-and-ball feet, *81*
coat closet from doorstops, *103*
Colonial style, *94*
commissions, *14–15, 33*
commode, *147*
construction
    of case goods, *47–48*
    cushions, *38–40, 64–65*
    of frames, *34–36*
    springs, *37–38*
contracts with designers, *13–15*
Cooper Hewitt Design Museum, *107*
Corbusier, Le, *93, 97*
cork furniture, *130–132*
cottage style, *127–129*
couches
    price factors, *63–65*
    proportions, *108–109*
Cressent, Charles, *87*
Criard, Mathieu, *87*
CS Post, *104*
cupboards, *80*

cushions, *38–40, 64, 65*
custom pieces, cost of, *12–13*
cutouts, *81*

D

Danhauser, Josef, *96, 148*
Danish furniture, *150*
DAR chair, *149*
dealers
    asking questions of, *5–6*
    judging customers, *9–10*
    negotiating price with, *4–5*
decorating
    on a limited budget, *100–108*
    reference materials, *101*
delivery times, *24–25*
deodorizing antiques, *27–28*
design centers, *7–9, 23–24*
designers. *See* furniture designers;
interior designers
desk lamps, inexpensive, *105–106*
discounts, asking for, *4–5*
dovetailing, *66*
drawers, *48, 66, 67*
dressers, *65–67*

E

Eames, *97, 149*
Eames plywood chair, *149*
Egg chair, *150*
English furniture styles
    Arts and Crafts, *84*
    Chippendale, *81*
    English Regency, *82–83*
    Georgian, *81*
    Queen Anne, *80*
    Victorian, *83–84*
    William and Mary, *79–80*
English library sofa, *148*
English Regency furniture, *82–83*
EQ3, *139–141*

F

fabric covers, *40–41, 59*
fabric quality, *63*
fabric safety, *43*
façades, *56*
finishes, *48–49, 56–57, 58*
finishing touches by top designers,
112–114
flea market shopping, *102, 104,
110–111*
floral carvings, *79–80, 81*
Fontaine, Pierre, *90*
formaldehyde, *51*
frames, *34–36, 64–65*

Franklin Report, *101*
French 1940s style, *134–136*
French Empire style, *90–92*
French furniture styles
    Art Deco, *93*
    Art Moderne, *93*
    Art Nouveau, *92*
    French Empire, *90–92*
    French Provincial, *90*
    Louis XIII, *85*
    Louis XIV, *85–86*
    Louis XV, *87–88*
    Louis XVI, *88–89*
French Provincial style, *90*
furnishing entire house, *19–20*
furniture designers
    Adam, Robert, *81*
    Allison, Amy, *119–121*
    Almada, Jorge, *132–134*
    Benneman, G., *89*
    Bertoia, *97*
    Biedermeier, *96*
    Breuer, Marcel, *97, 148, 161*
    Chareau, Pierre, *93*
    Chippendale, Thomas, *81, 147*
    Corbusier, Le, *93, 97*
    Cressent, Charles, *87*
    Criard, Mathieu, *87*
    Danhauser, Josef, *96, 148*
    Eames, *97, 149*
    Fontaine, Pierre, *90*
    Godwin, Edward William, *83–84*
    Guimard, Hector, *92*
    Hays, Tyler, *121–123*
    Hepplewhite, *81*
    Hiltl, Josef, *148*
    Holland, Henry, *83*
    Horta, Victor, *92*
    Jacob, Georges, *88*
    Jacobsen, Anne, *150*
    Kutash, Noleen, *124–126*
    Maine Cottage Furniture, *127–129*
    Majorelle, Louis, *93*
    Michalik, Daniel, *129–132*
    Midy, Anne-Marie, *132–134*
    Morris, William, *83, 84*
    Nash, John, *83*
    Percier, Charles, *90*
    Phyfe, Duncan, *95*
    Ponti, Gio, *97*
    Pugin, Augustus, *83*
    Riesener, Jean-Henri, *88–89*
    Ruhlmann, Jacques Émile, *93*
    Saarinen, Eero, *97, 150*

Schinkel, Karl Friedrich, *96, 148*
Serrurier-Bovy, Gustave, *92*
Shapiro, Richard, *134–136*
Sheraton, Thomas, *81, 82–83*
Spector, Laura, *137–139*
Stickley, Gustav, *84, 95*
Tielmann, Peter, *139–141*
van de Velde, Henry, *92*
van der Rohe, Mies, *97, 149*
Volpe, Steven, *142–143*
Webb, Philip, *83–84*
Wright, Frank Lloyd, *95*
furniture styles
American
American Federal, *95*
Colonial, *94*
Mission, *95*
Shaker, *94*
English
Arts and Crafts, *84*
Chippendale, *81*
English Regency, *82–83*
Georgian, *81*
Queen Anne, *80–81*
Victorian, *83–84*
William and Mary, *79–80*
French
Art Deco, *93*
Art Moderne, *93*
Art Nouveau, *92*
French Empire, *90–92*
French Provincial, *90*
Louis XIII, *85*
Louis XIV, *85–86*
Louis XV, *87–88*
Louis XVI, *88–89*

G
gateleg table, *146*
George IV, King, *82–83*
Georgian furniture, *81*
German furniture style, *96*
glides, *66*
Godwin, Edward William, *83–84*
Gregory, John
decorating advice, *106*
finishing touches by, *112*
Guimard, Hector, *92*

H
hand-rubbed finishes, *49*
Hansen, Fritz, *150*
hardware
authenticating antiques, *56*
exposed, *84*

hardwood frames, *34–36*
Hays, Tyler, *121–123*
Hedge, *142–143*
Hepplewhite, *81*
hidden expenses, *18–19*
highboys, *80, 145*
high-gloss finishes, *49*
Hiltl, Josef, *148*
hinges, *48*
Holland, Henry, *83*
Horta, Victor, *92*

I
IKEA, *105, 111, 115, 141*
interior designers
Alexandriuk, Kim, *100, 105, 109, 111, 112*
backgrounds of, *100*
Bell, Robin, *103–104, 105, 108*
billing arrangements, *13–14*
Branca, Alessandra, *105, 106, 109, 110, 113*
choosing, *11–12, 101, 114–115*
contracts with, *14–15*
fees of, *14–15, 111–112*
Gregory, John, *106, 112*
imagination and taste of, *16–17*
Joyce, Kerry, *104, 106, 110–111, 112–113*
mark up custom pieces, *12–13*
Redd, Miles, *102–103, 106, 110, 113*
Robinson, Harriet, *106, 110, 113*
role of, *10–11*
Romano, Todd Alexander, *105, 106, 108*
Smith, Travis, *102, 108, 109, 110, 111, 113*
Stanton, Lee, *107, 111*
Volpe, Steven, *106, 111, 113–114*
Watts, Willis, *104, 107, 110, 113*

J
Jacob, Georges, *88*
Jacobsen, Anne, *150*
joinery, *47–48, 66, 67*
Joyce, Kerry
decorating advice, *104, 106*
finishing touches by, *112–113*

K
knobs, *48*
Kutash, Noleen, *124–126*

L
lacquer finishes, *49, 79–80*
latticework, *81*
Le Brub, Monsieur, *86*
leather furniture, *41–43, 84*

Lee's Studios, *106*
legs
    American Federal style, *95*
    Art Deco style, *93*
    Biedermeier style, *96*
    block style, *95*
    cabriole, *81, 87*
    column style, *88*
    construction of, *64*
    Georgian style, *81*
    Louis XIII style, *85*
    Louis XIV style, *85*
    Louis XV style, *87*
    Louis XVI style, *88, 89*
    Mission style, *95*
    square, *88*
    straight, *85, 95, 96*
    tapered, *89, 96*
    twisted, *85*
library table, *147*
lighting sources, *105–106*
Lightology, *106*
Ligne Roset, *105*
Louis XIII style, *85*
Louis XIV style, *85–86*
Louis XV armchair, *147*
Louis XV style, *87–88*
Louis XVI style, *88–89*

M
mahogany, *81, 83*
Maine Cottage Furniture, *127–129*
Majorelle, Louis, *93*
Malmaison, *92*
Manufacture Royale des Meubles de
la Couronne, *86*
Michalik, Daniel, *129–132*
Midy, Anne-Marie, *132–134*
Mission style, *84, 95*
Mitchell Gold, *104*
Modern Movement style, *96–97*
Morris, William, *83, 84*

N
nails, *47*
Napoleon and Josephine, *91–92*
Nash, John, *83*

O
oak, *84*
online shopping, *108, 109–110*
organic furniture, *49–51, 53*

P
padding variations and price, *64*
paint, decorating with, *102–103*

particle board case goods, *45–46*
Percier, Charles, *90*
period furniture. *See also* antiques
    ancient times, *76*
    19th century, *77–78*
        American Federal, *95*
        Art Nouveau, *92*
        Biedermeier, *96*
        French Empire, *90–92*
        French Provincial, *90*
        Mission, *95*
        Shaker, *94*
        Victorian, *83–84*
    17th and 18th centuries, *76–77*
        American Federal, *95*
        Chippendale, *81*
        Colonial, *94*
        English Regency, *82–83*
        French Provincial, *90*
        Georgian, *81*
        Louis XIII, *85*
        Louis XIV, *85–86*
        Louis XV, *87–88*
        Louis XVI, *88–89*
        Mission, *95*
        Queen Anne, *80*
        Shaker, *94*
        William and Mary, *79–80*
    20th century
        Art Deco, *93*
        Art Moderne, *93*
        Art Nouveau, *92*
        Arts and Crafts, *84*
        Modern Movement, *96–97*
Phases Africa, *124–126*
Phyfe, Duncan, *95*
plywood case goods, *45*
plywood frames, *36*
polyurethane, *51*
Pompadour, Madame de, *87–88*
Ponti, Gio, *97*
price
    in design centers, *23–24*
    negotiating, *4–5, 22–23*
    researching before buying, *73–75*
    value related to, *32–34, 52–53, 61–70*
Pugin, Augustus, *83–84-84*

Q
Queen Anne chair, *146*
Queen Anne furniture, *80–81*
questions, asking of dealers, *5–6*

R
R&Y Augousti, *105*

Redd, Miles
  decorating advice, *102–103, 106*
  finishing touches by, *113*
reference materials, *101*
reproductions, vs. antiques, *25–27*
Restoration Hardware, *105, 106*
retail stores, experts' favorites, *107*
Retro style, *96–97*
return policies, *18*
Riesener, Jean-Henri, *88–89*
Robinson, Harriet
  decorating advice, *106*
  finishing touches by, *113*
Rococo style, *87–88*
Romano, Todd Alexander
  auction bidding advice, *108*
  decorating advice, *105, 106*
royals, related to furniture, *75–76*
Roycroft Industries, *84, 95*
Ruhlmann, Jacques Émile, *93*
rustic style, *84, 137–139*

S

Saarinen, Eero, *97, 150*
Schinkel, Karl Friedrich, *96, 148*
scrolls, *79–80*
secretary, *145*
selecting furniture, *32–34, 51–53. See also* case goods; upholstered furniture
Serrurier-Bovy, Gustave, *92*
Shaker style, *94*
Shapiro, Richard, *134–136*
shell motifs, *80*
Shelter, *104*
Sheraton, Thomas, *81, 82–83*
shipping charges, *19*
shopping online, *108, 109–110*
sideboards, *81*
Smith, Travis
  antiques shows advice, *111*
  decorating advice, *102, 109*
  finishing touches by, *113*
solid wood case goods, *45*
Spector, Laura, *137–139*
springs, *37–38, 64*
Stanton, Lee
  antique buying advice, *107*
  antiques shows advice, *111*
staples, *35, 36, 47*
steel frames, *36*
steel furniture, *148, 149*
Stickley, Gustav, *84, 95*
StudioLo, *134–136*
styles. *See* furniture styles

T

table decorations, *102*
Tielmann, Peter, *139–141*
timetable for decorating, *100–101*
Troscan Design, *119–121*
Tulip chair, *150*

U

upholstered furniture. *See also* legs
  construction quality, *64–65*
  cushions, *38–40, 64, 65*
  fabric covers, *40–41*
  fabric quality, *63*
  first appearance of, *79–80*
  frames, *34–36, 64–65*
  Georgian style, *81*
  leather, *41–43*
  price factors, *63–65*
  purchasing guidelines, *52*
  red velvet, *83*
  selection tips, *39*
  springs, *37–38, 64*
  used, *104*

V

van de Velde, Henry, *92*
van der Rohe, Mies, *97, 149*
veneers, *46–47, 53, 65, 67*
Versailles, *86*
Victorian furniture, *83–84*
Visual Comfort, *106*
Vogel, Joshua, *122*
Volpe, Steven
  antiques shows advice, *111*
  biography and inspiration, *142–143*
  decorating advice, *106*
  finishing touches by, *113–114*

W

walnut, *79–80, 83*
warranties, *17–18*
Watts, Willis
  antique buying advice, *107*
  decorating advice, *104*
  finishing touches by, *113*
Webb, Philip, *83–84*
West Elm, *111*
William and Mary furniture, *79–80*
Williams-Sonoma Home catalog, *106*
Windsor chair, *146*
wing chairs, *79–80*
winged-back chair, *146*
wood floors, covering for, *103–104*
woods, *55–56*
Wright, Frank Lloyd, *95*

Photo Credits

Cover:

Black Chippendale style chair with red cushion
Atelier Branca
Chicago, IL
(312) 787-6123
abranca@branca.com

Chest, chaise lounge chair, egg chair,
Barcelona chair and highboy
Leslie Hindman Auctioneers
Chicago, IL
(312) 280-1212
www.lesliehindman.com
Julie@lesliehindman.com

Cork chair
Daniel Michalik
Providence, RI
(401) 952-5579
www.danielmichalik.com
danielmichalik@mac.com

Directoire-style stool (on Jennifer's hand)
Jessica Tampas Photography, Ltd.
Chicago IL
(312) 942-1905
www.jessicatampas.com

Lamp
Noleen Kutash for Phases Africa
Los Angeles, CA
(949) 721-9661
www.creativedetailing.com
Noleen@creativedetailing.com

Interior:

Sketches
Amy Allison for Troscan Design
Chicago, IL

(312) 733-0158
www.troscandesign.com
amy@troscandesign.com

North America's Ten Best Newly Discovered Furniture Designers:

Amy Allison
Chicago, IL
(312) 733-0158
www.troscandesign.com
amy@troscandesign.com

Tyler Hays for BDDW
New York, NY
(212) 625-1215
www.bddw.com
info@bddw.com

Noleen Kutash for Phases Africa
Los Angeles, CA
(949) 721-9661
www.phasesafrica.com
Noleen@creativedetailing.com

Maine Cottage
Yarmouth, ME
(888) 859-5522
www.mainecottage.com
info@mainecottage.com

Daniel Michalik
Providence, RI
(401) 952-5579
www.danielmichalik.com
danielmichalik@mac.com

Anne-Marie Midy and Jorge Almada for Casamidy
San Miguel de Allende, Mexico
011 + 52 (415) 152-0403
www.casamidy.com
Casamidy@casamidy.com

Richard Shapiro for StudioLo
Los Angeles, CA
(310) 275-6700
www.rshapiroantiques.com
Richard@rshapiroantiques.com

Laura Spector for Laura Spector Rustic Designs
Fairfield, CT
(203) 254-3952
www.lauraspectorrusticdesign.com
lsrustic@aol.com

Peter Tielmann for EQ3
Division of Palliser Furniture
Winnepeg, Canada
(204) 954-7070
www.eq3.com
info@eq3.com

Steven Volpe for Hedge
San Francisco, CA
(415) 357-1102
www.hedgegallery.com
info@hedgegallery.com

About the Author

Jennifer Litwin, a graduate of the University of Chicago Graduate School of Business, is a consumer reporter and contributing writer for *Consumers Digest* magazine, where she selects the magazine's "Best Buys" in the furniture category. She is also the author of *Furniture Hot Spots: The Best Furniture Stores and Websites Coast to Coast.* Litwin has been featured in numerous publications, including the *Boston Globe, Miami Herald, Atlanta Journal-Constitution, Seattle Times, Times-Picayune, San Francisco Chronicle, USA Today,* and *National Enquirer.* She has also given numerous speeches across the country on furniture-related topics, and has appeared on numerous television programs as a consumer reporter.